Contents

152,453

List of Forms

Chapter Nine

Chapter Ten

Appendix

Preface

I'm never sure what to say when people ask how long it took to write this book. Many of the ideas were ones I explored when I taught elementary school in Colorado and Washington for nine years. My graduate work focused specifically on children's literature, teaching writing, and authentic assessment. I received my master's degree from the University of Colorado in 1982, and my doctorate from the University of Washington in 1991. I am currently an adjunct professor in the graduate programs at Seattle Pacific University and Seattle University. Many of the ideas from this book arose from talking with and observing outstanding teachers in my work in schools. I also worked as a consultant with the Bainbridge Island School District for three years, offering workshops, teaching courses, and facilitating grade level meetings. The writing of this book was part of a three-year process of change in that district. Bainbridge Island is a half-hour ferry boat ride directly west of Seattle, Washington. With an island population of 17,000, the district consists of approximately 3,500 students in one high school, one middle school, and three elementary schools.

This book is the direct result of several reading and writing classes and two courses on authentic assessment. Together, we explored the topics, read a great deal, and began developing our own assessment tools and techniques. Many elementary teachers on Bainbridge Island assisted in various stages of this book, from participation in classes, to the development and piloting of the forms. A dozen teachers worked intensively on this book, revising forms and writing portions of the text. These teachers are true "reflective practitioners" and I learned a tremendous amount from them.

I worked on the text for this book while Cindy Ruptic helped refine and design the forms on the computer. Cindy has taught elementary and secondary school for 22 years. For the past year, she has been teaching a multi-age primary classroom on Bainbridge Island and next year will be teaching in Osaka, Japan. Since this was a collaborative venture, the term "we" is used throughout the book. Our collaboration has been a fine example of classroom/university partnership.

Bonnie Campbell Hill

Note: Permission is granted to reproduce the forms in the book for classroom use only. If the forms are included in other publications, credit must be given and permission granted from the publisher.

Acknowledgments

We would like to acknowledge all the elementary teachers in the Bainbridge Island School District who participated in the development, piloting, and revision of these forms. We specifically thank those teachers who worked intensively on individual chapters.

In addition to working on the forms, Cindy Ruptic helped a great deal with Chapter 4 on organizing portfolios and the two chapters on observing reading and writing growth. Patti Kamber contributed to the four chapters on organizing portfolios, content area assessment, involving students in the assessment process, and the chapter on evaluation and reporting. Her gift for encouraging student reflection is incredible. Carrie Holloway shared many of her forms and worked on Chapters 9 and 13. Jan Peacoe was our expert on involving special students and assessing reading growth. Roz Duthie was our resident kindergarten authority and contributed to the chapter on observing emerging readers and writers, as well as the chapters on writing and reading assessment. Jan Colby helped write portions of the chapter on emerging readers and writers and Chapter 11 on involving parents in assessment. Cindy Fulton helped with Chapter 5 on observing students and Chapter 8 about observing reading growth. We'd also like to thank the following teachers who contributed to specific chapters: Babs Brownell (Chapter 7), Roger Sater and Dana Boren-Swisher (Chapter 8), Mary Hadley (Chapter 9), Karin Torgerson (Chapter 10), and Sandi Sater (Chapter 13).

All of these teachers gave us reactions to forms and reviewed drafts. This book is a testimonial to these teachers' hard work and professionalism. Although we tried diligently to credit the author of each form, we gained many ideas by reading books and sharing with other colleagues. We thank all who participated in our professional dialogue about assessment and evaluation. The contributors decided that part of the royalties from this book will go to a fund that the elementary teachers on Bainbridge Island can use for professional growth in the area of assessment.

We also appreciated the valuable support and advice Lisa Norwick and Dr. Nancy Johnson offered. A special thanks to our friend and mentor, Dr. Sam Sebesta, whose feedback and seal of approval we treasure.

Although we dread sounding like the Academy Awards, we want to acknowledge the hard work of our editor, Sue Canavan. She walked us through the process and was always supportive and encouraging. We appreciate her trust and confidence in the project. Warren Freeman's eye for a stray comma or unnecessary word was a delight. We also appreciated the pats on the back and helpful suggestions of Dr. Jean Church, Carol Hasson, Debbie Davis, Bill Walseth, Julie Aegerter, Dr. Carol Santa, and Dr. Mina Bayne who reviewed our manuscript.

Our most heartfelt thanks, however, go to our families, who put up with our long hours on the computer and our absorption with forms and portfolios. Our husbands, Steve and Woody, provided us with a great deal of technical and emotional support. We'd like to dedicate this book to Cindy's daughter, Rosemary, and Bonnie's three children, Keith, Laura, and Bruce, who were patient and understanding about the many days and hours consumed by "The Book."

B.C.H.
November 1993

CHAPTER ONE

Framing the Puzzle

This is not an ordinary book. *Practical Aspects of Authentic Assessment: Putting the Pieces Together* is an interactive text. We've designed the text and the forms to be used flexibly. Assessment is currently a hot topic, but most recent books remain at the theoretical level. Our focus in this book is on specific and practical aspects of assessment and evaluation in elementary classrooms. This book is not only about portfolios, but about collecting and recording information from multiple sources on an ongoing basis. Changing curriculum and assessment techniques takes a great deal of time and hard work. Making forms, especially on the computer, is very time consuming, so we've included over 120 reproducible forms in this book.

OVERVIEW

In the first two chapters, we explore the philosophy behind portfolios and authentic assessment and evaluation. We then address more practical concerns by describing three stages of the process: getting started, getting comfortable, and fine-tuning. Chapter 4 provides information on how to organize portfolios and diagnostic information. In that section, we show a glimpse of how one particular teacher uses portfolios in her classroom. The next chapter briefly focuses on observing students and organizing anecdotal records.

The middle four chapters of the book include assessment tools and forms for specific areas: emergent literacy, writing, reading, and content areas. We've developed assessment forms for developmental spelling, writing conferences, reading logs, literature circles, problem solving, and many more. Each technique or tool is described briefly and we've included blank forms as well as a few completed samples.

In Chapters 11 and 12 we discuss the role of the students and families in assessment and evaluation. In the next chapter, we suggest ways to involve specialists and students with special needs in the process. The last two chapters help fit all these pieces together by addressing evaluation and reporting, including descriptions of continuums, parent conferences, and progress reports.

The forms in this book were developed by teachers and have been used in their classrooms. They evolved through many drafts as teachers read and shared ideas with students and colleagues. These discussions about curriculum and assessment created a new sense of community and professionalism. The Index of Forms after the Table of Contents lists the 123 forms included in this book. If the forms are included in other publications, credit must be given and permission granted by Christopher-Gordon Publishers. Otherwise, we encourage you to photocopy and adapt the forms in the book for your personal classroom use.

We chose not to delve into issues of why standardized tests are inadequate measures of student growth or the need for other forms of assessment. Other authors (Anthony, et al.,

1991; Rhodes & Shanklin, 1993; Shepard, 1989; Tierney, et al., 1991) have explored these issues at great length. As Chittenden (1991) observes,

> When students leave school, they are judged for the rest of their lives by the quality of work they produce and the quality of personal skills they possess, not by their ability to take tests. If I want students to put their full hearts into becoming better workers and more thoughtful people, then it is their work and effort that must be the basis of assessment." (p. 35)

This book is intended for those who are interested in alternative assessment and ready to begin "putting the pieces together."

NOTE TO ADMINISTRATORS

Principals and language arts specialists work with teachers who have a variety of backgrounds and expertise in curriculum and assessment. Administrators need to validate teachers, yet also nudge and invite them to grow as professionals. There is a fine line between encouraging and mandating change! The challenge is for administrators to become involved alongside teachers in learning, reflecting, and decision-making so that the staff feels a sense of ownership in the changes.

This book provides practical information for teachers who are just getting started, getting comfortable, or fine-tuning their assessment program. *Practical Aspects of Authentic Assessment* may help administrators clarify issues and support teachers at all stages of growth. Changes in assessment and evaluation are part of a long-term process that requires time and thrives best with administrative support.

WHERE ARE YOU IN THE PROCESS?

Those of you who are just getting started may find it easiest to begin by focusing on a particular area such as writing. Others may wish to choose three or four techniques or components as a starting point for change. It is important that your choices are consistent with your philosophy and reflect the kinds of activities your students are already doing. Stop there! Work on implementing those few techniques until you and your students feel comfortable with both the forms and the criteria for evaluation. Feel free to adapt the forms until they fit your needs. You may wish to skim the first two chapters before adding another piece to your assessment program. Take it slowly so that neither you nor your students become frustrated or overwhelmed. Remember, change takes time.

If you've already begun using portfolios and authentic types of assessment, the first three chapters of this book may serve as a review. You've probably read some books and articles, attended workshops, or taken an alternative assessment class. Use the index or "menus" from Chapter 3 to note the forms you're already using. You may wish to adapt the forms from our book. We recommend that you use each form with your students before tackling new forms and techniques. We'd also urge you to include your students in creating and evaluating forms. Involving students in the assessment process is the next step for many teachers. A word of caution: it's easy to start drowning in forms at this point, so be selective.

Some of you have been experimenting with portfolios and holistic assessment for quite some time. As you fine-tune your own forms, we invite you to continue our professional dialogue by sending us copies of your forms either as hard copy or on a disk. You can send materials to: Dr. Bonnie Campbell Hill, c/o Christopher-Gordon Publishers, Inc., 480 Washington Street, Norwood, MA 02062.

STARTING THE PUZZLE

Three years ago, none of us could have imagined becoming passionate about assessment. Our enthusiasm grew as we worked late at school and on weekends, and met at night to develop and revise these tools. The process of sharing our insights revitalized and enhanced our teaching. We wanted to share our work and our excitement with other teachers. This is the book we wish we'd had when we began. We wanted to fill in some of the "missing pieces" by focusing on the *practical* aspects of classroom assessment. We hope this book will provide a scaffolding for you as you continue your own exploration of assessment and evaluation. We certainly do not claim to have "solved" the puzzle. We would like to share with you the products and process of working collaboratively as we struggled to develop a holistic picture of teaching, learning, assessment, and evaluation.

What are your beliefs about teaching and learning? What are your goals for your students? Based on your philosophy and curriculum, how can you best measure what your students are learning? Based on the information you gather and insights you gain, how will you adapt your teaching to better meet the needs of your students? These are the questions that must precede any discussion of alternate assessment techniques. In the next chapter, we explore how changes in assessment are inextricably interwoven with changes in philosophy and curriculum.

CHAPTER TWO

Getting the Whole Picture

It's hard to put a puzzle together unless you've seen the complete picture. It helps when you keep the box propped up in front of you in order to keep looking back and forth between the individual pieces and the whole picture. For most of us, changes in assessment came about because of changes we were making in philosophy and curriculum. Problems occur when administrators and teachers hear about portfolios and decide to jump in without having spent considerable time dealing with philosophy, goals, and curriculum first. This "cart before the horse" approach often results in frustration and misunderstandings about portfolios and authentic assessment.

Figure 2-1 illustrates how changes in assessment and evaluation are part of a larger picture. Portfolios and authentic assessment are based on a holistic, responsive, and child-centered curriculum. We placed the child at the center of the figure to emphasize the notion that our decisions must be based on the ages and populations with whom we work. The arrows extend in both directions since students' responses can affect decisions about curriculum, assessment, and evaluation. We also want to emphasize the recursive nature of the process; changes in any one area may affect other areas. We'll next briefly discuss each of the seven components in the circle.

PHILOSOPHY

Before you can begin to assess and evaluate learning, it's crucial to review, revise, and articulate your beliefs about teaching and learning. These beliefs should be grounded in current research on language and literacy development. Whether you are working individually, or as a school or district, the process of clarifying these beliefs is a vital first step. If your primary goal is to nourish active, independent learners who view learning as a lifelong process, then traditional report cards and standardized test results are simply inadequate.

The use of portfolios makes sense when a teacher, school, or district has made a commitment to a holistic view of learning and teaching. A holistic perspective is based on current research that highlights the interactive nature of speaking, listening, reading, and writing. This philosophy focuses on the whole child, including physical, social, and emotional, as well as intellectual growth. Once you've clarified your general beliefs about teaching and learning, you can formulate a more specific philosophy of assessment and evaluation.

Try to put your philosophy into understandable language so that you can use it with parents, students, and other teachers. As an example, on page 7 we included the Bainbridge

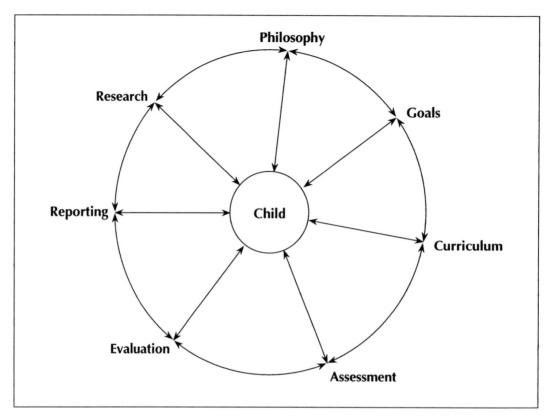

Figure 2-1   Putting the pieces together.

Bainbridge Island School District's Philosophy Statement on Assessment, Evaluation, and Reporting. This statement was developed after much discussion and revision involving all the elementary teachers in the district. The teachers plan to continually review this document so that all assessment and evaluation planning will be grounded in a common philosophy.

GOALS

Once you have articulated your beliefs, the next step is to define your specific goals as a district, school, or individual teacher. Since this book is written primarily for classroom teachers, we've included a form (on page 9) for defining your own philosophy and goals. This process could also work for district or building inservices. We realize that divisions by content areas are arbitrary and some teachers may simply wish to write goals for their students as learners. It's important to try to be specific, yet focus on your most important values. Your challenge is to try to keep this list to one or two pages that you can share with parents and your school principal.

CURRICULUM

After you've defined your philosophy and goals, then you can focus on the specifics of your curriculum. Hopefully, all three components will mesh! Changes in the Bainbridge Island School District began with Language Arts. Their focus this year is on technology and math. It's frightening that curriculum development in some schools takes place in seven-year cycles

BAINBRIDGE ISLAND SCHOOL DISTRICT

Philosophy of Assessment, Evaluation, and Reporting

The ongoing assessment of student progress, meaningful evaluation of that progress, and reporting in a manner which communicates clearly between school staff, students, and parents are critical components of successful educational programs. The quality of information gained through assessment determines the quality of evaluation. Instructional and curricular decisions will be based on the data gathered through assessment and evaluation.

Therefore, assessment and evaluation must be centered in the classroom, tied directly to current curriculum, consistent with district goals, and consistent with what we know about learning. Assessment and evaluation must be comprehensive and include both objective measures and professional judgments about academic performance and personal growth. Reporting must reflect an educational program that teaches the whole child, preparing him/her to function in a rapidly changing world. The progress report is a summary of student growth and progress for each reporting period.

Core Beliefs

Parents and students should be clearly informed of areas to be assessed and expected student outcomes. Their active participation in the assessment and evaluation process is crucial.

Assessment, evaluation, and reporting focus on what a student can do and is trying to do, based on developmental benchmarks.

The quality of information gained through assessment determines the quality of evaluation and reporting.

Assessment, evaluation, and reporting procedures and instruments are selected based on identified district, building, classroom, and individual learner outcomes, learning opportunities and classroom practices.

Assessment, evaluation, and reporting are free of gender and cultural bias.

Assessment, evaluation, and reporting document development and improvement, and identify areas for growth.

Assessment, evaluation, and reporting use both objective measures and professional judgments about academic performance and personal growth.

Evaluation and reporting include information about the student processes, products and performances.

Student progress is reported in the context of the individual learner as well as in relation to typical performance for students of the same age or grade level. However, it is not a ranking system.

Informal reporting includes such activities as sending home examples of student work, informal exchanges, conferences, telephone calls, notes, anecdotal reports, and newsletters. The nature and frequency of this reporting are determined as the need arises. Informal reporting is recognized as essential in fostering successful home-school partnerships.

Formal reporting includes conferences and progress reports which are issued on a regularly scheduled basis.

Parents are encouraged and invited to respond and initiate communication in both the formal and informal reporting processes.

The heart of the Bainbridge Island philosophy is that learning is an ongoing developmental process, unique to each child. As teachers, our responsibility is to record what the child can do and the patterns of growth over time.

when textbooks are adopted; curriculum reexamination should be ongoing. Curriculum should be responsive to current children's literature, technology, and new research in education.

You may want to begin by listing your broad curricular goals on the form on page 9. Then, on the Curriculum and Assessment form on page 10, list the specific components of your program. For instance, your writing program may include writing workshop, mini-lessons, author's chair, and publishing. The components of a literature-based reading program may involve reading aloud, SSR, literature circles, dialogue journals, and response projects.

Deep level change is a long-term process and cannot occur during occasional half-day inservices or after-school meetings. To be successful, teachers need time for inservice, time to meet and share ideas, and opportunities for reading, writing, and observing colleagues.

ASSESSMENT

Assessment is the process of gathering evidence and documenting a child's learning and growth. Assessment is trustworthy and authentic when it occurs as a regular part of classroom learning and instruction. Assessment helps teachers plan curriculum and instruction in order to meet the needs of every student. Multiple measures are needed to collect information in a variety of contexts. Teachers collect anecdotal notes from conferences and observations, data from surveys and interviews, and samples of student work. Authentic assessment should mirror "real" as opposed to artificial literacy events. Here it's important to clarify the term "authentic" with a definition.

> In an authentic assessment, the student not only completes or demonstrates the desired behavior, but also does it in a real-life context. "Real life" may be in terms of the student (for example, the classroom) or an adult expectation. The significant criterion for the authenticity of a writing assignment might be that the locus of control rests with the student; that is, the student determines the topic, the time allocated, the pacing, and the conditions under which the writing sample is generated. (Meyer, 1992, p. 40)

It's important to articulate your purpose for assessment. Edward Chittenden (1991) suggests four purposes: keeping track, checking up, finding out, and summing up. He states, "The third assessment attitude or stance is, I believe, the most interesting and probably the most crucial to successful teaching . . . The find-out stance is fundamental to the success of the sort of decentralized and process-oriented curriculums now being advocated in many places" (p. 30). He goes on to suggest that this stance of inquiry is the "framework for responsive teaching." In this book, we place a heavy emphasis on observing, talking with students, and involving them in the assessment process.

We've briefly touched upon philosophy, goals, and curriculum and we've defined some terminology. Once you have your philosophical foundation in place, you can start deciding which specific assessment tools you will use. The rest of the book will focus on assessment tools and techniques.

At the top of the Curriculum and Assessment Form on page 10, you can write your broad goals for a particular subject, such as writing. In the left-hand box, list each specific focus. Next, list the components of your writing program. Opposite each component, note the specific assessment tools and techniques that you plan to use to assess student writing. We have provided one teacher's form for you as an example. This form may help you bridge the gap between instruction and assessment.

Philosophy and Goals

I believe people learn best when _____

_____

My role as a teacher is to _____

_____

The goal of all education should be _____

_____

By the end of the year, I hope that my students will _____

_____

My broad curriculum goals for this year are _____

_____

_____

My professional goals for this year are

_____

_____

_____

The purpose of assessment is to _____

_____

The purpose of evaluation is to _____

_____

In addition to progress reports, I will describe student growth using _____

_____

_____

Curriculum and Assessment

Goals:

Focus	Curricular Component	Assessment Tools or Technique

Comments, Goals or Changes:

Curriculum and Assessment

Goals:

Focus	Curricular Component	Assessment Tools or Technique
reading for fun! building fluency	D.E.A.R. (silent reading)	*reading log
reading growth		monthly tape of reading
understanding of elements of literature	Literature Circles	dialogue journals
discussion of literature		response projects
vocabulary and fluency development	Reading Conferences	anecdotal records
focus on effective reading strategies		reading folder forms (*)
		* interest survey
		* strategies I use
		* reading goals
focus on skills & comprehension		reading continuum
		retelling
		QRI / miscue analysis
fostering a positive attitude		reading attitude survey

Comments, Goals or Changes:

EVALUATION

Evaluation is the process of summarizing and interpreting evidence, and making professional judgments based on the information collected. Students should be evaluated on both their own personal growth, and in comparison to widely held expectations for a particular grade level or age group. This "stepping back," in order to value or reflect upon learning and progress, is what separates assessment from evaluation.

The choices you make about evaluation will depend a great deal on the policy of your school and district. Student evaluation will be determined to some extent by whether or not you are required to give grades and by the nature of your report card. Whatever the constraints, you can decide how assessment data and student portfolios can supplement and enrich your evaluation program.

We've found the previous two forms helpful in articulating our philosophy and goals. You may wish to complete these forms at the beginning of the year and then refer to them periodically. The information would be helpful to share with parents at Back to School Night and with administrators.

REPORTING

Reporting involves reflecting on what you know about your students, making instructional decisions, setting goals, and then sharing that information with students, parents, and administrators. In Chapter 11, we discuss a variety of methods for involving parents in the evaluation process. Because the distinction between assessment, evaluation, and reporting is often unclear, we've provided a visual representation of the terms in Figure 2-2.

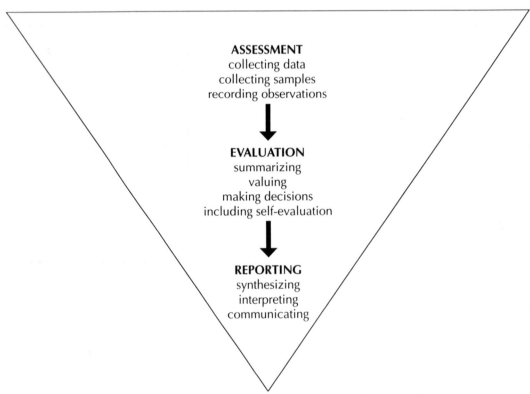

ASSESSMENT
collecting data
collecting samples
recording observations

EVALUATION
summarizing
valuing
making decisions
including self-evaluation

REPORTING
synthesizing
interpreting
communicating

Figure 2-2   Visual representation of the distinction between assessment, evaluation and reporting.

RESEARCH

The information you report to parents should be based on observations, student work, and your experience as a teacher. In addition, your assessment and evaluation tools will be shaped by current research in education. In turn, you can share your insights by contributing to the growing body of qualitative, classroom-based research. Your research will affect your philosophy in the continual cycle of learning and teaching.

ARTICULATING BELIEFS, GOALS, AND PLANS

On the next set of pages, you'll see an example of one teacher's planning for his writing program. He first outlined his philosophy and goals for the writing program in his first-grade classroom. Next, he listed the main components of his program and the specific assessment tools or techniques that he planned to use to collect information about his students as writers. Finally, he added his own goals and a monthly timeline for collecting information about his students.

In this chapter we tried to show how philosophy, goals, curriculum, assessment, evaluation, reporting, and research are all woven together. We hope these are not empty exercises, but provide thoughtful ways of clarifying and sharing your values with students, colleagues, and the wider community. Articulating your beliefs, goals, and plans may help you keep the larger picture in mind before you begin putting the pieces together.

PHILOSOPHY

I believe children learn best when they are in a positive environment which allows them to make choices and grow in responsibility. Individual strengths are a major focus in this environment. Taking risks are encouraged and seen as a way of learning.

My role as a teacher is to promote this type of environment, facilitate learning, model learning, develop a knowledge about my students, and provide the appropriate materials and resources.

By the end of the year, I hope that my students will continue to be excited about learning, be able to work cooperatively, and have an understanding about their own abilities as readers and writers.

The purpose of assessment is to collect data and record observations pertaining to specific goals. This data will help determine the next direction of curriculum instruction. Evaluation occurs as I analyze the collected data and observations and reflect upon students' growth over time. Assessing and evaluating are best utilized when interactions between student, parents, and teacher take place on a regular basis. This plan will address how I plan to assess students while involving them and their parents.

PROFESSIONAL GOAL

This year, I will work more on assessing students by taking anecdotal notes, conducting surveys and/or interest inventories, and having students self-reflect on their work. Students will keep portfolios (a sample of their work). Throughout the year, I will work on giving students ownership of their portfolios by having them determine some of the contents of the portfolios as well as having them learn to analyze their work.

LITERACY GOAL #1

> **Students will learn reading strategies and comprehension skills through a literature-based reading workshop.**

Curricular Components	Assessment Tools
• As beginning 1st graders, students will demonstrate literacy knowledge.	• Concepts about Print test.
• Students will be accountable for relaying their learning to others (specifically, parents).	• Weekly Summaries
• Parents will receive specific information regarding their child's progress in reading and writing.	• Report Cards • Reading Continuum
• Students will synthesize literature by creating appropriate response activities. Students will be able to verbalize why they made certain choices in regard to specific activities.	• Literature Response Projects
• Students will spend time in silent reading.	• Reading Log
• Students will demonstrate greater fluency in reading.	• Videotape • Miscue Analysis

The following components will be assessed informally through the use of anecdotal notes. Later in the year additional assessment may be added.

- Read-alouds
- Literature Circles
- Listening to books on tape
- Mini-lessons focused on reading strategies.

LITERACY GOAL #2

> **Students will learn to make choices and develop responsibility as they explore the writing process.**

Curricular Components	Assessment Tools
• Students will share their individual interests with classmates and teacher. As the year progresses, students will be encouraged to write about their interests during writing workshop.	• Interest Inventory
• Students will demonstrate growth in spelling and editing.	• Writing Sample/ Fix-it

- Students will be accountable for relaying their learning to others (specifically parents).

- Students will be accountable for their time during writing workshop and will be encouraged to try new steps of the writing process as they require it.

- Parents will receive specific information regarding their child's progress in reading and writing.

- Words I Can Spell List
- Weekly Summaries

- Status of the Class Checklist

- Report Cards
- Writing Continuum

The following components will be assessed informally through the use of anecdotal notes. Later in the year additional assessment may be added.

- Message Board
- Calendar
- Graphs
- Content Area Learning Logs

THESE ARE SOME THINGS I'M ALREADY DOING THAT I WILL CONTINUE

Report Cards

Literature Response Projects

Reading Log

Videotape Students Reading

Status of the Class Checklist

Limited Anecdotal Notes

Miscue Analysis

THESE ARE SOME THINGS I'M PLANNING TO BEGIN IN THE FALL

Concepts about Print Test

Weekly Summaries

Reading Continuum

Writing Continuum

Interest Inventory

Writing Sample/Fix-it

Words I Can Spell List

Daily Anecdotal Notes (1 note per child per week)

THESE ARE SOME THINGS I'D LIKE TO IMPLEMENT SOON

"Me as a Writer and Reader"

Friday Folder

Photos of Sample Products

Running Record

Parent Survey

CLASSROOM TIMELINE

September

Concepts about Print Test

Interest Survey

Videotape

October

Writing Sample (save for later in year)

Begin Weekly Summaries

Status of the Class Summary

Videotape

November

Report Cards

Reading Continuum

Writing Continuum

Literature Response Project

(& Self-Reflection)

Reading Log

Writing Sample (& Self-Reflection)

Videotape

December

Status of the Class Summary

Videotape

January

Consider beginning Friday Folders

Videotape

February

Writing Sample/Fix-it

Status of the Class Summary

Videotape

March

Report Card

Reading Continuum

Writing Continuum

Literature Response Project

(& Self-Reflection)

Reading Log

Writing sample (& Self-Reflection)

Videotape

April

Status of the Class Summary

Videotape

May

Writing Sample/Fix-it

Videotape

June

Report Card

Reading Continuum

Writing Continuum

Status of the Class Summary

Literature Response Project

(& Self-Reflection)

Reading Log

Writing Sample (& Self-Reflection)

Videotape

CHAPTER THREE

Putting the Pieces Together

When you put a puzzle together, do you first find the edge pieces? Then do you sort by color or shape? Do you start with the most recognizable parts of the picture, the sections that stand out, or your favorite color? How you begin putting the puzzle of assessment together will be different for each of you, depending on your needs, experience, and personal style.

The first section of this chapter, Getting Started, will describe how some teachers begin moving toward authentic assessment by collecting student work. The next section, Getting Comfortable, provides some ideas about how teachers can initiate portfolios by asking students to select representative samples of work in all areas of the curriculum. The third section, Fine-Tuning, reveals how teachers can encourage student reflection and involvement in the portfolio process. There are quite a few references to forms and tools that we describe in more detail in later chapters; however, we wanted to first describe the process of collection, selection, and reflection.

GETTING STARTED: COLLECTING

Let's imagine you're in a fairly traditional school and you've been teaching awhile, but you're a bit uncomfortable about how neither standardized tests nor the report card really reflect how your students are doing as readers and writers. You've just started using literature to supplement your reading program and you've begun having your students do more writing. How can you document the growth and excitement your students are showing about reading and writing to your principal and parents?

One of the first things you probably do when working on a puzzle is collect the pieces and turn them all over. One simple way to move toward authentic assessment is to start collecting samples of student writing. We've found it's easier to start with writing for two reasons. First, it's fairly straightforward to collect information since writing involves a tangible product. Second, writing instruction doesn't seem to carry the emotional or curricular weight that typifies reading instruction. Most teachers have been given very little guidance on how to teach writing. Traditional reading instruction, on the other hand, comes laden with detailed curriculum guides and extensive reading texts and workbooks.

Writing Folders

Donald Graves (1983) and Lucy Calkins (1986) describe a workshop approach to teaching writing, including the use of Writing Folders where students date and collect drafts of writing.

Some teachers use two folders: one for ongoing pieces of writing, and one for published pieces, old drafts, and abandoned writing. If children are writing daily, whether in kindergarten or in 5th grade, the writing soon starts to pile up.

One kindergarten teacher on Bainbridge Island, Jan Colby, gives her students a "journal" every week with five pieces of paper stapled together. Starting on the first day of school, her five- and six-year-olds write, scribble, or draw about whatever they choose. There is a stamp on each table so the children can date each page. At the end of the week, Jan gives each student a "Post-it" note, and asks the children to mark their favorite piece of writing. Each Friday she asks the children to tell her why they chose that particular piece of writing. She then transcribes their responses directly onto the "Post-it" note as she roves around the room. The students' insights reveal much about what children value ("I picked it because it's funny") and the ways in which they are constructing meaning. She then has a parent photocopy the page each child marked, write the child's name, and file the page in the child's Writing Folder. The journals then go home with the proud kindergartners at the end of the week. This basic Writing Folder is a first step toward the use of portfolios.

Using this method, each kindergartner has a Writing Folder with a sample from each week of school. Sparked by ideas in *Joyful Learning* (Fisher, 1991), Jan also developed a method for involving her young students in self-reflection. At parent conference time, Jan calls each child up for a five minute conference sometime during the day. She spreads the writing samples out on the desk in the order they were written, and asks the child, "What do you notice?" As the child remarks on the changes in content and development (i.e., "I am a better draw-er now."), Jan records the conversation on a piece of paper. She later takes her notes and transcribes them into a letter to parents, called "We Noticed." At conferences, Jan greets each parent with this joyful letter, accompanied by samples of the child's writing. For example, in the fall, Jan wrote, "Sally and I noticed that she likes to draw with lots of different colors. She likes to write and draw and tell about animals and her friends in her stories. She has made a lot of new friends." By March, Jan's comments reflect Sally's increase in writing skills and strategies, as well as her developing metacognitive awareness: "Sally says she notices how she can write some 'real words' now. Sometimes she uses the sounds of letters to figure it out, and sometimes she says she just 'knows it in her head.' Sally says she likes being an author." We've included a copy of Jan's "We Noticed" form in Chapter 11.

The important thing about Jan's system is that it's organized and she doesn't have to do a great deal of additional work. She isn't the one pulling samples each week. Her assessment process is part of her daily teaching. Her structure also provides her young students with opportunities for self-reflection.

Teachers of older students may also choose to use Writing Folders. In Chapter 7, we have included samples of forms that we staple to the four sides of each student's writing folder:

1. Topics
2. Skills I Know
3. Pieces I've Written
4. Goals

Writing Folders may also contain self-assessment forms, such as the ones listed in Chapter 10. As the teacher and students look at representative samples, they can evaluate the writing and set goals together.

All of a student's writing from the quarter or trimester probably won't fit in one folder. Most teachers have two places for student writing. The Writing Folder usually includes the piece or pieces a student is currently writing. Students can store other work in a folder in a filing cabinet or hanging file. These Storage Folders should always be accessible, so students can go back to earlier writing they may wish to revisit or revise.

You may want to involve students in deciding what to call the daily and storage folders.

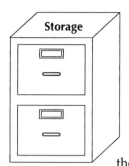

Some teachers have upright boxes to house four to six daily folders for each table to prevent traffic jams. Other practical matters to consider are the size of folders; they must be big enough to hold large pages if your students write on oversized paper. It's important to set up a clear system that works well for you and is easy for students. You might want to start slowly and role play procedures with younger students. The easier the system is to use, the more likely you will use it regularly.

Finally, you need to decide where published pieces of writing are to go. Are books and projects filed in the Storage File or displayed in the room? Are they sent home "for good?" Have you put library pockets in student-authored books, along with a few blank pages for comments? You should revisit the philosophy and goals of your writing program. If you mainly use journals and worksheets, a Writing Folder doesn't make much sense. If, on the other hand, your students are writing regularly, you need some manageable way to collect representative samples and not drown in paperwork. We'll talk more about assessing and evaluating writing in Chapters 6 and 7.

Reading Folders

Once you've started collecting writing samples in a Writing Folder, you may want to start a Reading Folder with similar forms:

1. Interest Survey (Chapter 10)
2. Reading Log (Chapter 8)
3. Strategies I Use (Chapter 8)
4. Goals (Chapter 7)

The information from the interest survey may be useful in helping students find books. Students can record the books they are reading, their responses to literature, and the reading strategies they are learning. You can meet with each student to define his/her goals for the upcoming term.

Teacher's Notebook

The information in a Student's Portfolio, however, is not the only information you have about a child. You probably collect diagnostic information and anecdotal notes about students throughout the year. The information you gather can help in making decisions about curriculum, instruction, evaluation, and reporting to parents. Many teachers maintain a Teacher's Notebook with pages for each student. A Teacher's Notebook becomes a place where you can record diagnostic information about oral reading and reading conferences, notes about contact with parents, and emergency numbers. You may also have a grade book and files for each student where you keep results from standardized tests and progress reports. You could keep some items, such as attitude or interest surveys, either in your Teacher's Notebook or the Reading/Writing Folders, depending on the ages of your students.

The teachers involved in writing this book selected six books, listed chronologically, that they found most helpful in getting started. Although only one of these deals specifically with assessment, each author presents ways to document growth and assess learning more holistically. These books have been around for a few years now, but we constantly refer to them and strongly urge you to read one or two. These were some of the most significant books that inspired our changes in curriculum and led us into the use of portfolios and authentic assessment. We've also included a "menu" of reading and writing "ingredients" which may provide a structure for beginning to use portfolios.

REFERENCES FOR GETTING STARTED

Calkins, Lucy. (1983). *Lessons from a Child: On the Teaching and Learning of Writing*. Portsmouth, NH: Heinemann. Lucy Calkin's book provided one of the first glimpses of a conference approach to teaching writing. Calkins follows one child's writing development over several years.

Graves, Donald. (1983). *Writing: Teachers and Children at Work*. Portsmouth, NH: Heinemann. This book revolutionized the teaching of writing around the world. It doesn't have all the answers, but it raised many questions and launched other researchers. Graves is a key figure and his book is a classic.

Clay, Marie. (1985). *The Early Detection of Reading Difficulties*. Portsmouth, NH: Heinemann. A new edition of this book is forthcoming. Marie Clay is a prominent researcher in diagnosis and instruction. She provides detailed instructions on the administration and scoring of many assessment techniques such as miscue analysis, running records, and strategies for determining a child's emerging concepts about print.

Calkins, Lucy. (1986). *The Art of Teaching Writing*. Portsmouth, NH: Heinemann. If you want to buy one book on how to begin using a process approach to teaching writing, this is it. Teachers find this book practical and full of rich examples. It was a significant book for all of us.

Atwell, Nancie. (1987). *In the Middle: Writing, Reading, and Learning with Adolescents*. Portsmouth, NH: Heinemann. This was a landmark book that every middle and high school teacher should read. Atwell's book has done more to transform writing at the intermediate level than any other book. Her work with adolescents is convincing and inspiring.

Goodman, Ken, Goodman, Yetta & Hood, Wendy. (1989). *The Whole Language Evaluation Book*. Portsmouth, NH: Heinemann. This was one of the first books published on authentic assessment. The caliber of the chapters is uneven, yet the voices of teachers attempting to integrate assessment with instruction at all levels were a breath of fresh air. Yetta Goodman states that their book seeks to "legitimize the power of the professional intuition of teachers" (p. 5).

GETTING STARTED MENU OF ASSESSMENT TOOLS AND TECHNIQUES

STUDENT PORTFOLIO

General Information

Interest Survey

Writing

Writing Attitude Survey
Writing Samples
Writing Folder Forms

Reading

Reading Attitude Survey
Reading Log
Reading Folder Forms

TEACHER NOTEBOOK

General Information

Family Information (phone numbers, etc.)
Anecdotal Records

Writing

Writing Conference Forms/Notes

Reading

Reading Conference Forms/Notes

GETTING COMFORTABLE: SELECTING

Writing Folders and Reading Folders are strong first steps, but a collection of work samples is not a portfolio. The difference between folders and portfolios is the process of selection and reflection. Although the next chapter delves into the portfolio process in more depth, we want to begin here with a definition.

A portfolio is an organized collection of student work and self-reflections that helps paint a portrait of the whole child. The systematic process of collecting, selecting, and reflecting upon learning is what makes a portfolio dynamic and meaningful. Our definition will change as we explore the potential by developing portfolios alongside our students.

As teachers first begin to use portfolios, they sometimes start drowning in paperwork. Collecting is not enough! As you become more comfortable with collecting information, you will want to involve students in selecting and reflecting on representative samples. Moving from collection to selection is a major step for both students and teachers. At this stage you and your students should wrestle with the issue of quality and the criteria for selection. The "ingredients" described in the next few pages involve selection and reflection by students. You'll need to spend considerable time talking with students about the rationale and criteria for selection. We'll describe more about this process in Chapter 4.

Writing

The most powerful way to document writing growth is for children to collect and date writing samples in their Writing Folders. During writing conferences, you can note new skills and risk-taking. In addition, you can also look at writing growth over time by photocopying a fall sample of a student's work. Give the copy to the student in May, saying, "Show me what you've learned." Using this "Fix-It" strategy, students correct spelling, add punctuation, and make revisions. Children are often unaware of how much they are changing. Parents and teachers who see children every day may also fail to recognize how far students have come. The "Fix-It" technique can help students and families celebrate growth.

Teachers may also want to incorporate a spelling attitude survey or give children a list of 10 predetermined spelling words. Without studying those words, give the same list in the winter, and again at the end of the year, noting the changes in the students' spelling development. We've included these forms and techniques in Chapter 7 on Observing Writing Growth.

Reading

In the area of reading, a simple next step is to regularly tape record students reading. After practicing their selection, older students or adult volunteers can help primary students record their names, the date, and the title and author of the pieces they read. Once students understand the procedure, you can set up your listening center so that children could independently tape record their reading. You may want to make a copy of the text and record the children yourself in order to do an informal Miscue Analysis. Older students may choose to select a passage or poem to read with expression.

Videotapes provide even richer information. Depending on your community, you could ask families to provide a blank tape. The students could take the tapes home at the end of the year. Your schools might be willing to purchase one audiotape or videotape per child that would travel with the student each year until the student leaves the school.

Students can include samples from dialogue journals, photographs, or videotapes of literature response projects. Each quarter children may also want to include a page attached to their reading logs, justifying two favorite books from the quarter. The more comfortable you become with portfolios, the wider the range of data you and the students may decide to include. We describe each of these techniques in detail in Chapter 8, called Observing Reading Growth.

Content Areas

You can widen the scope beyond reading and writing by focusing on learning in other content areas. You could incorporate photographs or samples of student work from science, health, social studies, and math in student portfolios. Videotapes provide a wonderful way to capture learning, especially for students with different learning styles. Chapter 9 further explores Assessment in Content Areas.

Diagnostic Information

One way to learn a great deal about students is to keep written notes about children's comments, insights, and behaviors. These anecdotes, or vignettes, provide specific clues about how children learn. In Chapter 5, we focus specifically on different ways to organize anecdotal records. We've discovered that taking anecdotal notes is valuable, as long as the process isn't too time-consuming.

You may also wish to keep other diagnostic information in your Teacher's Notebook, such

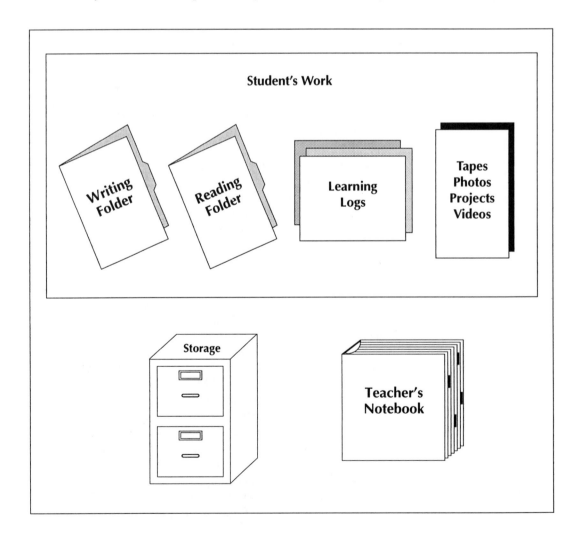

as an informal miscue analysis or running record. You can summarize the results from such tools in progress reports and during conferences. These evaluations should form the basis for decisions about instruction. As more teachers begin to move away from decontextualized measures, such as multiple choice tests and grades, we hope that educators and parents will begin to see the value of authentic assessment strategies that occur during daily classroom activities.

On the previous page, we've tried to show graphically how the collection of student work, the Storage Files, the Teacher's Notebook, and the Student Portfolio fit together. We have also listed books that we found helpful as we grew more comfortable with authentic assessment. Finally, we've included a broader "menu" of options for portfolios and your Teacher's Notebook. No teacher will incorporate every item; this list is intended only as a list of possibilities. We hope you will add more of your own!

REFERENCES FOR GETTING COMFORTABLE

Routman, Regie. (1988). *Transitions: From Literature to Literacy*. Portsmouth, NH: Heinemann. Routman's persuasive book includes practical ideas about how to begin shaping a whole language classroom and how to begin the transition toward a literature-based reading program. The appendix provides a wealth of resources.

Harste, Jerome, Short, Kathy & Burke, Carolyn. (1988). *Creating Classrooms for Authors: The Reading-Writing Connection*. Portsmouth, NH: Heinemann. Here is the book with the "nitty gritty." It includes pages of detailed information on Author's Chair, Author's Circles, shared reading, and an introduction to literature circles. Teachers still refer back to this very practical book.

Rhodes, Lynn & Dudley-Marling, Curtis. (1988). *Readers and Writers with a Difference: A Holistic Approach to Teaching Learning Disabled and Remedial Students*. Portsmouth, NH: Heinemann. This book contains specific strategies for helping learning disabled and remedial students with the reading and writing processes. Special education and Chapter I teachers will find the details in this book inspiring and practical.

Fisher, Bobbi. (1991). *Joyful Learning: A Whole Language Kindergarten*. Portsmouth, NH: Heinemann. Kindergarten teachers spend a great deal of their time watering things down and figuring out how to assess two classes of emergent readers and writers. Fisher's book provides helpful ideas for changes in both curriculum and assessment in kindergarten.

Harp, Bill (Ed.). (1991). *Assessment and Evaluation in Whole Language Programs*. Norwood, MA: Christopher-Gordon Publishers. Bill Harp's book is a collection of articles on assessment in various classrooms. It includes chapters on authentic assessment in intermediate classrooms, bilingual classrooms, and special education classrooms. The suggestions for record keeping and self-evaluation are particularly valuable.

Tierney, Robert, Carter, Mark, & Desai, Laura. (1991). *Portfolio Assessment in the Reading-Writing Classroom*. Norwood, MA: Christopher-Gordon Publishers. This easy-to-read book provides the best overview of portfolio assessment. Although it leaves many questions and gaps, this is a perfect book for teachers just beginning to use portfolios.

FINE-TUNING: REFLECTING

For many of you, the pieces in the puzzle are already beginning to fit together. One issue that often plagues teachers at this stage is the question of criteria. It's important to focus on student growth over time, but how can we know the student is growing at an appropriate rate for his/her age? What is acceptable? What are our standards? How do we evaluate as well as assess growth? We address these questions in greater detail in Chapter 13; however, we will briefly discuss the concept of benchmarks and the role of students.

GETTING COMFORTABLE MENU OF ASSESSMENT TOOLS AND TECHNIQUES

STUDENT PORTFOLIO

General Information

Interest Survey
Parent Survey
Self-Portrait

Writing

Writing Attitude Survey
Writing Samples
Writing Folder Forms
"Fix-It" Writing Samples Fall/Spring
10 Words Over Time (Spelling)
Spelling Attitude Survey

Reading

Reading Attitude Survey
Reading Log
Reading Folder Forms
Audio/Videotapes of Reading

Content Areas

Photographs or Samples of Projects
(math, science/health, social studies)

TEACHER NOTEBOOK

General Information

Family Information (phone numbers, etc.)
Anecdotal Records

Reading

Reading Conference Forms/Notes
Simplified Miscue Analysis

Writing

Writing Conference Forms/Notes

Celebrating Growth

In order to evaluate student learning, we must return to our philosophy, goals, and curriculum. When teachers first begin collecting information, it's often too difficult to focus on criteria at the same time. We found we first had to gain a real sense of what children could do and become skilled observers before we could recognize, articulate, and document the patterns we saw at particular stages of growth.

The teachers on Bainbridge Island developed a Reading and Writing Continuum based on current research and their experience as teachers. The descriptors from these continuums then became part of instruction, assessment, and evaluation. Several teachers are now beginning to work on math and science continuums to parallel what they have done in language arts.

If a portfolio represents a glimpse of one year, how can we capture growth and change over a longer period? Teachers on Bainbridge Island also developed a Learning Profile as a kind of mini-portfolio, containing representative samples from each year. The Learning Profile will follow students from kindergarten through fifth grade. We describe both the Continuums and the Learning Profile in Chapter 13.

Involving Students in the Process

The second issue that quickly surfaces in any discussion of portfolios is the question of ownership. It is our belief that a portfolio is a portrait of a student and belongs to the student. You may initially decide how to begin implementing portfolios, but it's important to involve the students as much as possible (see Chapters 4 and 10). Tierney et al. (1991) state:

> We have found that when given the opportunity, it is the students who are the most perceptive judges of their own work because it is the students who best know the intricacies involved in the formulation of the portfolios . . . Assessment is not an isolated responsibility for the teacher, but a collaborative effort designed to inform not only the teacher's instruction, but also the students' learning. As such we believe that it is essential to involve the students in actively developing criteria and assessing their own portfolios. (p. 175)

Involving students in setting criteria and evaluating progress is challenging, but highly rewarding. When students set the criteria for evaluation, the expectations become clear and students have a sense of ownership. It is important that students understand why information is being collected and how it will be used. At the elementary level, incorporating student voice in evaluation feels a bit like showing our underwear! Until recently, grading and evaluation have been mysterious, hidden processes that teachers "did to students." Do you remember carrying home a sealed manila envelope with your report card wondering, even dreading, what was inside? Even after it was opened, were you clear about the difference between an "A" and an "A-" or a "B-" and a "C+"? Children have been left outside the assessment and evaluation process for far too long. If portfolios truly belong to students, we need to respect their decisions and listen to their voices about what they are learning and what is important to them. In her work with middle school and high school teachers, Roberta Camp (1992) noted,

> It seemed to us, therefore, after four years of experimenting and refining, that the first steps toward creating a portfolio would need to engage students in simple and non-threatening forms of reflection while providing ample support and building a climate of trust. The early stages would involve teacher modeling and oral reflection. (p. 65)

You may want to begin to ask students what they want to include in a portfolio. Students can help develop the "menu" of choices, which may vary each trimester. Depending on the grade level, you can ask students to include a "Post-it" note, index card, or form for each component in their portfolio. Their portfolio entries might include brief process notes, a description of the pieces, and a self-reflection. It may be helpful to write a monthly summary when you review portfolios with students. Finally, you may want to develop a system for including peer and parent comments in the portfolios. We explore these ideas further in Chapters 10 and 11.

Donald Graves and Bonnie Sunstein, in their inspiring book, *Portfolio Portraits* (1992), urge teachers to start keeping their own portfolio. When we've kept portfolios ourselves, we became more determined to incorporate aspects of ourselves as learners outside the classroom. Some children may be outstanding pianists, artists, or athletes outside school, and yet those interests and talents may not be reflected in their portfolios. If portfolios belong to a student and reflect the whole child, then we need to develop ways to incorporate and invite a wide range of components.

As we've looked back at our own growth in the area of assessment and evaluation, we see a pattern: *collect, select, reflect*. We moved from collecting samples to selecting representative pieces to evaluate. As we grew in confidence, we asked students to help select work and asked them to reflect on their choices.

In the next chapter, we describe how one teacher involves her students in self-reflection and the specifics of how portfolios work in her classroom. She developed a way for students to regularly share their work with families, using what they call a Friday Folder. Every other week students take their work home in these folders, accompanied by a reflective letter, and parents add comments. The students bring their Friday Folders back and sort their work into either their Portfolio, their Working Folders, or the Storage File. In order to be dynamic, selection should be an ongoing process and students should constantly review and update their portfolios.

We've provided a final graphic representation of all the assessment components we've discussed in this chapter: folders of student work, Storage Files, Teacher's Notebook, the Student Portfolio, the Friday Folder, and the Learning Profile. The arrows show that student samples should constantly be reviewed and exchanged as students grow. Understanding how all these pieces fit together has been a tremendous help to teachers in implementing portfolios in their classrooms.

The "menu" on page 28 includes much more self-reflection than the previous two menus. Remember, this is not a list of what you should include in their students' portfolios; these are simply choices on a menu. No one could or would want to include everything. Much of what you decide to include will depend on your beliefs and the activities in your individual classroom. You may even vary the items from quarter to quarter. We hope you will involve your students in deciding what, how often, by whom, why, and when to include portfolio components. One of the most powerful articulations of the power of portfolios was Sheila Valencia's article in *The Reading Teacher*. The last three sentences of her article capture our beliefs about portfolios.

> Portfolios represent a philosophy that demands that we view assessment as an integral part of our instruction, providing a process for teachers and students to use to guide learning. It is an expanded definition of assessment in which a wide variety of indicators of learning are gathered across many situations before, during, and after instruction. It is a philosophy that honors both the process and the products of learning as well as the active participation of the teacher and the students in their own evaluation and growth. (Valencia, 1990, p. 340)

The list of books on the last two pages of this chapter includes the most recent and inspiring books we've found, arranged by publication dates. Our list keeps changing as new books on this topic flourish. Be warned, however, that several recent books on the market with the word *assessment* or *portfolio* in the title have been a disappointment. We've also listed a few publications from non-mainstream presses that were particularly useful in developing our forms and continuums.

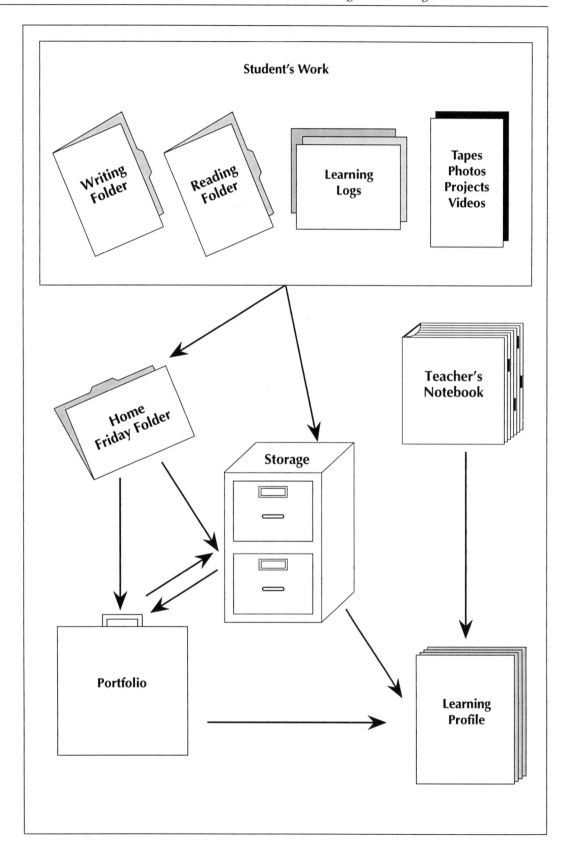

FINE-TUNING MENU OF ASSESSMENT TOOLS AND TECHNIQUES

STUDENT PORTFOLIO

General Information

Interest Survey
Parent Survey
Self-Portrait
Self-Evaluation of Portfolio Contents
Self-Evaluation Forms
Peer Evaluations
Monthly Teacher Reviews
Friday Folder Form

Writing

Writing Attitude Survey
Writing Samples
Writing Folder Forms
"Fix-It" Writing Samples Fall/Spring
10 Words Over Time (Spelling)
Spelling Attitude Survey

Reading

Reading Attitude Survey
Reading Log
Reading Folder Forms
Audio/Videotapes of Reading
Sample of Reading Response Project
Sample of Dialogue Journal
Sample of Literature Circle Evaluation

Content Areas

Photographs or Samples of Projects
(math, science/health, social studies)
Integrated Thematic Project Samples
    and Evaluation
Collaborative Project Samples
Content Area Attitude Surveys
Artwork

TEACHER NOTEBOOK

General Information

Family Information (phone numbers, etc.)
Anecdotal Records

Writing

Writing Conference Forms/Notes
Emergent Literacy Evaluation
Writing Continuum

Reading

Reading Conference Forms/Notes
Simplified Miscue Analysis
Running Record/Emergent Literacy Evaluation
Reading Continuum

REFERENCES FOR FINE-TUNING

Anthony, Robert, Johnson, Terry, Mickelson, Norma & Preece, Alison. (1991). *Evaluating Literacy: A Perspective for Change*. Portsmouth, NH: Heinemann. This is not a book for teachers who want practical ways to "do portfolios." It's a much deeper book and is the best one we've found that really digs into the theory and philosophy behind authentic assessment and evaluation.

Calkins, Lucy. (1991). *Living Between the Lines*. Portsmouth, NH: Heinemann. Calkins's latest book is an inspiring collection of insights, reflections, and examples of children's writing. Calkins worked with teachers to extend writing and reading programs into their students' lives. It's a reflective, thoughtful book that raises as many questions as it answers.

Routman, Regie. (1991). *Invitations: Changing as Teachers and Learners K-12*. Portsmouth, NH: Heinemann. Routman has widened the primary grade range of her first book to reach K-12 in this volume. Her book is affirmative and provides so much material that teachers return to it repeatedly. She has outstanding chapters on special needs students, integration, and evaluation. Routman includes letters to parents, lists of references, and children's literature, and forms for evaluation. Teachers reread sections, underline quotes, and treasure this book.

Stires, Susan. (1991). *With Promise: Redefining Reading and Writing for "Special" Students*. Portsmouth, NH: Heinemann. Special education and reading teachers sometimes find it challenging to maintain a holistic perspective. *With Promise* provides "soft persuasion" about how to integrate authentic instruction and assessment when working with "special students." The chapter on pull out versus inclusion models is particularly powerful. The poignant prologue by Tom Romano, called "Third Strike" is worth reading aloud in a staff meeting.

Graves, Donald & Sunstein, Bonnie (Eds.). (1992). *Portfolio Portraits*. Portsmouth, NH: Heinemann. If the numbers of "Post-it" notes was the criteria for a useful and thought-provoking book, this one would win overwhelmingly. This was the book we'd been waiting for which expanded our vision and inspired many of us to begin keeping our own portfolios.

Yancey, Kathleen B. (1992). *Portfolios in the Writing Classroom: An Introduction*. Urbana, IL: National Council of Teachers of English. This collection of articles focuses on the use of writing portfolios at the middle school and high school levels. The articles are practical and thought-provoking and the appendix contains an excellent annotated bibliography.

Bouffler, C. (1992). *Literacy Evaluation: Issues and Practicalities*. Portsmouth, NH: Heinemann. We have much to learn from teachers in other countries. This book describes assessment and evaluation practices in Australia, Canada and England that wrestle with issues of large-scale assessment and quality of student reading and writing. This book has many nuggets and will make you think.

Rhodes, Lynn (Ed.). (1993). *Literacy Assessment: A Handbook of Instruments*. Portsmouth, NH: Heinemann. This recent Heinemann publication is an extremely practical collection of specific tools and forms. It's an excellent resource for teachers who are already comfortable with the philosophy behind authentic assessment and now need the practical tools.

Rhodes, Lynn & Shanklin, Nancy. (1993). *Windows Into Literacy: Assessing Learners K-8*. Portsmouth, NH: Heinemann. We were thrilled to receive this book in the mail. As the companion volume to the handbook, it's a comprehensive examination of authentic assessment to date. At almost 500 pages, it's a bit daunting, but is very readable and provides a current, comprehensive look at literacy assessment.

(Note: These next four resources were invaluable to us when we developed our own continuums and assessment forms. They may be less familiar to you since they are not available from major publishers. Published in Alaska, Canada, and Australia, we found these books extremely helpful.)

Literacy Profiles Handbook: Assessing and Reporting Literacy Development (1990) and *English Profiles Handbook* (1991). School Programs Division, Ministry of Education, Victoria, Australia. The nine reading and writing "bands" in these documents provide a basis for evaluating students' literacy development. The two books are a "must" for teacher developing their own continuums and benchmarks. These are practical books that would be helpful in creating and recording information about children K-12. There is a discount for multiple copies. For more information, write TASA, PO Box 382, Fields Lane, Brewster, NY 10509 or call (914) 277-8100.

Supporting Learning: Understanding and Assessing the Progress of Children in the Primary Grades RB0018, (1992). Ministry of Education, 620 Superior St., Victoria, British Columbia, Canada V9B 2M4 (604) 356-2500. For ordering, call Crown Publishing at (604) 386-4636. This very small booklet provides an overview of curriculum and assessment in British Columbia and could be useful for parents or teachers. The focus is on the whole child—on academic, social, physical, and emotional growth. The continuums in this booklet are outstanding. The book is accompanied by two larger documents *Primary Program Resource Document RB0008 (1992)* and *Primary Program Foundation Document CG0279 (1991)*. These two volumes include specific forms and explanations of many tools, techniques, and ways to assess learning. At this time, *Supporting Learning* costs about $6 and the two documents are about $20 each. Their new books on reference sets for writing (RB0020 and RB0021) have just become available.

Language Arts Portfolio Handbook for the Primary Grades, Juneau School District, 10014 Crazy Horse Drive, Juneau, AL 99801 (907) 463-1967. Revised September 1993. The Juneau School District developed this handbook for primary teachers as they move toward holistic literacy instruction and assessment. The handbook includes aspects of instruction and guidelines for assessment techniques.

Literacy Assessment in Practice: Language Arts. (1991). Education Department of South Australia. Distributed in the United States by the National Council of Teachers of English, Urbana, IL. (800) 369-6283. Those of you who are fine-tuning your assessment program may find this description of assessment and evaluation in Australia thought-provoking. This book provides some wonderful information on examining the quality of effective reading and writing, as well as a framework for collecting information about students' literacy development.

CHAPTER FOUR

Organizing Portfolios and Assessment Information

Many of you are parents as well as teachers. Some of you may also be taking classes or working on your master's degree. One of the keys to juggling work, family, graduate school, exercise, reading, etc., is organization. In this chapter we've specifically focused on some suggestions for organizing the assessment data you collect for each student. It's easy to become buried in writing samples, projects, and forms unless you have thought through your system for organizing information and portfolios.

SELECTING ASSESSMENT TOOLS

The types of assessment tools and techniques you decide to use depend on many factors, such as your philosophy, your teaching experience, and your knowledge of authentic assessment techniques. Your choices will also be affected by the ages and backgrounds of your students and by the amount of support from your colleagues and principal.

You'll need to decide your purpose for each tool, how often you'll assess each child, and where you will store the information. You'll probably want to keep most diagnostic information in your Teacher's Notebook. Students can store representative work samples in their own portfolios. Other items, such as attitude surveys, could go in either place, depending on the ages of your students.

Lynne Rhodes and Nancy Shanklin (1993) suggest asking the first two questions about your choices of what to collect. We have added two additional questions.

1. What does the information tell you about the child's development?
2. How will this information help you make curricular/instructional decisions about the child?
3. How often and when will you collect the information?
4. Where will the information be stored?

PORTFOLIOS

Historically, many professionals, such as architects and artists, have used portfolios to showcase their work and record their achievements. Besides celebrating a student's polished pieces and range of work, portfolios can also document a student's learning process. A classroom portfolio is an organized collection of student work and self-reflections that helps paint a portrait of the whole child. The systematic process of collecting, selecting, and reflecting upon learning is what makes a portfolio dynamic and meaningful. Student portfolios can reflect both process and product and can provide you with helpful information for planning curriculum and instruction. Portfolios have the potential to incorporate the voices of students in the assessment process and to create a bridge between instruction and evaluation. Best of all, as Sheila Valencia (1990) suggests, a portfolio approach "resonates with our desire to capture and capitalize on the best each student has to offer; it encourages us to use many different ways to evaluate learning; and it has an integrity and validity that no other type of assessment offers" (p. 338).

After your students have been using portfolios for a while, you may want to ask them for a definition of the term. We've included a few of the definitions from several fifth-grade students, ranging from very concrete to a broader understanding of the concept.

Portfolio Definitions by Fifth-Grade Students

Port stands for portable, and folio is a group of papers, so portfolio is a portable paper holder.

A portfolio is something to store work in, so if you get a job, you can take your portfolio and show what kind of work you do.

A portfolio is somewhere I keep things I want to be able to look back on.

A portfolio is something that has things you did or made that you're proud of and that show the progress you have made.

A portfolio is a collection of work that you think you would like to keep and save for the rest of your life. Then when you're an adult, you can look back and see what you did when you were young.

A portfolio is a big or small folder with pages and pockets. It holds your best and most interesting work. It is for looking back on your work when you are old and so people can look through it and know more about you. I like portfolios because it is a very organized way of showing people your best work.

After working individually, the students developed a class definition of portfolios:

A portfolio is a colorful collection of a person's work that shows his/her thoughts, interests, efforts, and goals in many different environments. Portfolios help learners see how they think, feel, work, and change over a period of time. The collections are really important to the learner.

Portfolios can range from simple to very comprehensive systems. We described a progression of portfolio development in Chapter 3:

- writing samples
- writing and reading samples
- writing, reading, and content area samples
- writing, reading, and content area samples, self-evaluation forms, photographs of projects, attitude surveys, etc.

Portfolios become richer and more representative of learning as your students become more involved in the selection and evaluation process.

In his chapter called "Portfolio Definitions" in *Portfolio Portraits*, Seger (1992) claims:

Defining *portfolio* from such multiple notions would be like an early biologist trying to define *mammal* when presented with a whale, a human being, and a bat. Like *mammal* was at one time, *portfolio* is a linguistic placeholder whose meaning will develop through examination and reflection. (pp. 115-116)

Why Use Portfolios?

It is not surprising that the recent interest in portfolios has occurred at the same time as the recent movement toward whole language. As the teaching of reading and writing shifts from a fragmented, skill-based approach, educators are discovering the need to show evidence of broader aspects of students' knowledge and growth. The use of portfolios enables teachers and students to recognize children's strengths and growth over time. Students can focus on the process of learning by including samples from different points in time, multiple drafts, and notes from projects.

It's imperative that you think about the purpose of portfolios before plunging into collecting and storing student work. Portfolios can be used within a classroom or can be used for school, district, or state evaluation. For more information on large-scale portfolio evaluation, see pages 429–431 in *Windows Into Literacy* (Rhodes & Shanklin, 1993) and Chapter 9 in *Portfolio Assessment in the Reading-Writing Classroom* (Tierney et al., 1991). We believe that portfolios will look very different if they are examined outside the student's home and classroom. If the purpose of a portfolio is to evaluate a program, then students would be more likely to showcase their "best work" and most proficient samples. Knowing portfolios will be evaluated will greatly affect the types of work students choose to include. The purpose of classroom portfolios can be much broader than evaluation and will mirror your philosophy and goals. Your definition of the purpose of portfolios in your classroom may be a combination of several of the following:

To celebrate growth

To document learning

To highlight a student's "best work"

To reflect risk-taking and experimentation

To improve instruction

To share information with families and other teachers

To nurture students and foster a positive self-concept

To encourage self-reflection

To help in goal-setting

It's important to remember that portfolios are only one method for collecting information and sharing what we know about students. There is no "right way." We worry that portfolios will become institutionalized and even required, and consequently, loose their fluidity and flexibility. The use of portfolios isn't something teachers can "learn to do" in a half-day workshop, but should grow out of their beliefs about teaching and learning. Our understanding of portfolios will change as we become more comfortable with the process and clearer about our purposes and criteria.

Who Owns Portfolios?

When we began keeping our own personal portfolios, we were fascinated by the wide variety of approaches to assembling portfolios. One teacher who developed a portfolio for job interviews focused on her professional writing, photos of her classroom, and examples of student work. Her portfolio was colorful and portable. Another teacher's portfolio reflected her random style and consisted of a large briefcase filled with papers, favorite books, items that held special memories, and student writing. A third teacher divided his portfolio into sections (personal information, professional writing, poetry, etc.), with reflections about each entry on brightly colored paper. Each portfolio was unique and represented the personal and professional aspects of each teacher. They enjoyed the process and were delighted with the product.

> "Beginning a portfolio was so helpful! Now I know exactly how my kids will feel. Plus, after seeing mine, I think they will feel safer in taking some risks, especially with self-reflection." —Lynne

> "Going through the process of making a portfolio made me understand how difficult, challenging, and fun it is to organize and condense aspects of my life. I realized that my portfolio was not finished; it's something that will grow along with me." —Paula

What Do Student Portfolios Look Like?

You might invite parents and professionals who keep portfolios to visit your classroom. Although professionals usually keep their work in expensive leather folders, children can discuss what types of pieces people include and how they are displayed. Most classroom teachers don't have much money for materials, so student portfolios are most often constructed of tagboard or posterboard. Some teachers and students, particularly in the intermediate grades, prefer three-ring binders. The advantage to binders is that pages can be added and removed. The disadvantage is that it's difficult to include audio or video tapes and artwork.

Other teachers have purchased folders with pockets and stapled one inside the other to form four pockets. You can also open the folders (without staples in the middle) to the full 17

inches and punch holes on one side. Students can use yarn to tie four or five opened folders together to hold large paper, puppets, videotapes, and artwork. A disadvantage of this method is that the portfolios can become quite bulky and objects can slip out of the pockets. In addition, this kind of portfolio can be difficult for you or your students to take home. You might want to share these options, then let students decide which format best meets their needs and reflects their personalities. By involving students in deciding what portfolios will look like and how they will be organized, students are practicing important decision-making strategies.

What Do Portfolios Include?

Portfolios often include samples or pictures of projects showing what students can do in a natural learning environment rather than in an artificial testing situation. As children develop as writers, it makes sense to include pieces of actual writing. As children learn to read, their growing competency can be documented by an audiotape and logs of the books they read. Students can add photographs of social studies and science projects. Your class might also want to include items that reflect their interests outside of school, such as music or sports. The more comfortable you and your students become with the portfolio process, the more types of data you may wish to include. You may want to start with a few items, adding a few more each term. It's helpful to focus on "significant" as well as "best" pieces. You will find that students often learn more by reflecting upon work that was a challenge or that provided new insights.

How Can Students Be Involved in Portfolios?

Portfolio collections are natural outlets for reflective thinking by learners. The key is "to keep portfolios fluid, changing, and responsive—and to keep the students at the center" (Milliken, 1992, p. 44). If portfolios are to be viewed as a learning tool as well as a way of reporting growth, then students need a voice in the process.

Students are capable of making reflective decisions about what they want to include in their portfolio. If we are trying to help students understand what they know at a metacognitive level, we must encourage them to think about what is important about the pieces they select. "Why did you select these pieces?" "What do they show me about you as a reader, a writer, and a learner?" Even very young children can address such questions and explain in their own terms the significance of each piece of work. Teachers of young children can transcribe these reflections to include with each component in the portfolio.

This process doesn't happen spontaneously, however. It takes a while for students to learn to trust their own judgment and standards. You may want to begin by asking them to select a piece that is important or their best work, and then asking them to explain their reasoning. Most children have relied so much on outside judgment about their work that these first steps require some patience on your part. Having work samples and self-reflections from past students has been a powerful tool for modeling self-reflection and self-evaluation. Prompts can also be very effective in the initial stages of self-reflection. You can remove the scaffolding of the prompts as students internalize the process. Here is Lisa Norwick's list of prompts that her students use when writing reflections.

- What is the process you went through while creating this piece?
- Who or what influenced you to create this piece?
- What risks did you take?
- What new knowledge did you gain?
- Why was this piece an experiment for you? What did you learn?
- Why did you choose this piece for your portfolio?
- Do you have any questions about this piece?
- If you were going to redo this piece, what would you do differently next time?

You will probably want to develop your own list with your students. We describe more about involving students in assessment and evaluation in Chapter 10.

When Do Students Reflect and Modify Portfolios?

When and how do students access, add, and delete items from their portfolios? Teachers need to provide the time and organization for such thinking to occur. The students will need time to write reflections about their entries. When we've kept our own portfolios, we discovered how much better our reflections were when they were done after a project, rather than in retrospect. You may decide to meet with students to formally review portfolios each month or each grading period. You'll also need time to informally confer about why they add some components and remove others. Later in this chapter, we'll describe how students can add and delete entries in their portfolios on a regular basis.

When Do Parents See Student Work?

Some teachers worry about not sending writing home. If writing goes home, however, the writers can't go back to work on it or look at growth over time. One solution is to have students select representative samples occasionally to photocopy and send home. Copying work can be a big job and there are often long lines in front of the school copy machine. Many of your decisions will also be affected by such practical constraints as limited paper budgets. Some options might be using parent volunteers, asking the PTA for funds, or applying for a grant. Some schools or districts that mandate the use of workbooks have allowed flexible funding, where individual schools or teachers can use a comparable amount of money to purchase literature and paper supplies instead of workbooks.

Most families are curious about what their child is learning in school. You can encourage parents to visit the classroom any time to see their child's portfolio. Classroom activities and samples of work can also be shared and celebrated through weekly newsletters, at Authors' Nights and Curriculum Nights, and through Friday Folders.

Depending on your population and the students' ages, you may also want to send student work home on a regular basis. Lisa Norwick, an intermediate grade teacher, sends the actual portfolios home once a month for parent review and response. On the next page, we've included a copy of her monthly letter to parents. Initially we worried that if students misplaced or lost their portfolios, important work from the entire year might be lost. Our fears were assuaged after seeing the care Lisa's students took of their portfolios. They had such a sense of ownership and pride that no one's work was handled carelessly. The decision whether or not to send portfolios home will depend a great deal upon the ages and population of your students. As parents, we'd love the opportunity to see work samples on a regular basis and to have an ongoing avenue for dialogue with our child's teacher.

Class Portfolios

Some teachers keep a class portfolio of significant projects, units, trips, and guests. The class portfolio provides a way for you to model how to collect, select, and reflect upon portfolio entries. Students can take pictures, write captions, draw sketches, and collect post cards to illustrate the myriad of things that happens in the classroom. Former students love to spot friends and siblings in class portfolios from previous years. The differences between a class portfolio and a scrapbook are the steps of selection and reflection. As a group, you would first need to decide the purpose of your class portfolio. Students would then have to decide how to organize the portfolio and what to include. They would also need to include a reflection about each entry.

Monthly Portfolio Letter

Dear Parents,

While you look at my portfolio with me, please notice these things:

These are some of the things I do well:

These are some of the things I am working on:

Please make a positive comment about my portfolio.

Organizing Student Portfolios

You may find yourself overwhelmed by the number of items each student has collected. Collections may include both polished and "in-process" pieces of writing, tapes of oral reading, journal samples, math projects, learning logs, and samples of work from content areas. The immediate problems are storage and selection.

You need a systematic, comprehensive way to organize work samples that presents a portrait of a learner's growth over time. How can you and your students decide not only what goes into the portfolio, but also how often to make additions or deletions? Which items will show another teacher or a parent what is essential about each student? How can the contents of a student's portfolio be clearly organized without becoming overwhelming?

Although portfolios are living, changing collections, there are some elements that may become more permanent either by requirement, design, or desire. A systemized list of portfolio components serves both as an organizational structure and as a guide for readers of the portfolio. Invite students to participate in decisions about what to include in portfolios as well as the criteria for evaluation.

In *Portfolio Portraits* (1992), Linda Rief describes how she decides the *external* criteria for what her eighth graders need to include in their portfolios, and how her students determine the *internal* criteria:

> I impose the *external* criteria for the portfolios—each student's two best pieces chosen during a six-week period with all the rough drafts that went into each piece, trimester self-evaluations of process and product, each student's reading list, and a final reading-writing project. The students determine the *internal* criteria—which pieces, for their own reasons. (p. 45)

Patti Kamber and her fifth-grade students developed their list of external criteria together. The Portfolio Components Checklist on the next page includes a list of items they felt would best represent their growth as learners and meet district requirements. Each grading period, students date their entries in the appropriate column. In reality, however, you'll probably find the list of components will change throughout the year as all of you become more confident about your choices and more comfortable with the process. The more students are involved in defining and planning portfolios, the greater their sense of ownership. We hope this simple form will serve as a springboard for you to develop your own checklists with your students.

How Can Portfolios Be Evaluated?

Our goal should be to help our students learn to evaluate their own growth. Donald Graves (1992) warns:

> There's a danger that portfolios may be evaluated the way I evaluated the writing of my students all those years ago. We'll evaluate the students' portfolios, curse their lack of ability to judge and improve their own work, then choose what work they ought to include. Fortunately, some professionals believe their students can learn to evaluate their own work effectively and make good choices for their portfolios. An emphasis on student evaluation, however, is slow going and tough work. (p. 85)

Our job as teachers is to help students learn the language for reflection, and to help them become aware of their own learning styles, patterns, and processes.

How do we evaluate portfolios? We can talk with students regularly about the components they are including and what they are learning by the process. We can respond periodically to their portfolios in writing and during student-parent conferences. Students can reflect

PORTFOLIO COMPONENTS CHECKLIST

Name: Teacher: Year:

Dates:			**PERMANENT**
			Progress report and Continuum
			Literature Logs
			Journals
			3 Peer Comments
			3 Parent Comments
			Monthly Teacher Reviews
			DYNAMIC
			*3 Pieces of fiction
			*3 Pieces of non-fiction
			3 Literature circle responses/debriefings
			*3 Math samples
			*3 Science pieces
			*3 Social Studies pieces
			*3 Samples of collaborative projects

*   Indicates pieces which must be accompanied by process notes, a description of the piece, and a self-reflective note.

PORTFOLIO COMPONENTS CHECKLIST

Name:			Teacher:	Year:

Dates:			**PERMANENT**
			DYNAMIC

* Indicates pieces which must be accompanied by process notes, a description of the piece, and a self-reflective note.

upon each entry and the portfolio as a whole. If you need to assign letter grades, you can help students set the internal and external criteria for evaluation for each component. If you decide to "grade" the portfolios themselves, you will find that students are more prone to focus on final polished products. They may be less candid and less likely to include examples of risk-taking. In addition, the focus will shift from a student-owned portfolio to a teacher/product centered collection of products.

Patti Kamber, whose classroom we will describe next, stresses, "Assessment within the portfolio needs to *capture and capitalize on the best each student has to offer*, rather than criticizing or finding errors. Assessment and evaluation should celebrate growth and inform instruction."

DESCRIPTION OF PORTFOLIOS IN ONE CLASSROOM

After hearing and reading about portfolios, many teachers want to know specifically what portfolios look like and details of the steps involved in instigating portfolios in the classroom. In this section we will present a detailed description of portfolios in one fifth-grade classroom.

Patti Kamber does a great deal of preparation with her students before they actually start making and using portfolios. At the beginning of the year Patti invites parents who use portfolios professionally to bring their work to school. Artists, cartoonists, architects, and anthropologists display a wide range of portfolios. Patti's students spend a great deal of time talking about how best they can show what they are learning through portfolios. She helps the students develop a purpose for their portfolios to ensure that decisions about the contents will be appropriate. Patti writes, "The purpose affects the design, the content, the link to instruction, and student motivation." This year the purposes for portfolios that she developed along with her students were as follows:

1. To nurture and develop a positive self-concept in the child and to promote lifelong learning.
2. To illustrate growth. Portfolios can illustrate growth by including a series of dated examples of actual school performance that show how the student's skills have improved over time. Changes on work samples, interest inventories, reading logs and journals are ways to illustrate growth. By reviewing their work, students develop the art and science of assessing their own learning.
3. To set goals. Goals are set by evaluating work from the student's portfolio. Goals are recorded during portfolio conferences. Other goals are taken from the curriculum and district objectives in relation to the individual child. These learning goals are addressed in the self-reflections and student/teacher reviews.
4. To provide an avenue of communication. Students, parents and the teacher can discuss the student's learning through parent conferences, Friday Folders, parent responses, and Parent Portfolio Nights.

She helps the students develop a list of items that they want to include in their portfolios. At the beginning of the year, the list is very open, consisting mostly of "Choose whatever is important to you and tell why." By the first grading period, students begin selecting representative work from many areas. The list changes as the students discover more about portfolios and their own learning processes. The power of portfolios comes when students use self-reflection and the criteria developed by the class to make decisions about what they want to show about themselves and why.

Friday Folders

Patti and her students keep personal learning logs where they record classroom activities and what they are learning. Besides reading and writing process folders, her students also have a

Friday Folders

Date	Initials	Comments for Teacher:	Comments for Your Child:
9/23	J.R.	Great literature program! Nate is excited about the choice of his books! How much time are you feeling is good for Nate to read each night?	I love your self-portrait! The words you used to describe yourself are right on! You're always fung smiles to see faces with your writing!
10/11	J.R.	Wow! Nate's editing really improved. Highly motivating math project! He worked hard last weekend — his choice ☺	Your description of the feeling trip made me feel like we were there again! You really worked hard on your math project — it turned out fantastic!
10/21	J.R.	I'd love to come in and help with the play. I can help with lines or props. Nate's excited about the U.S. trip.	Wow! You learned the location of all 150 states! What an amazing guy. I do not think I could do alone that without peeking. Your U.S. trip sounds fun!
11/3	J.R.	We love the weekly letters they help us know what to ask besides "How was school today?" See you at conference!	Nate, we are amazed at all the work you do each week.

Friday Folders

Date	Initials	Comments for Teacher:	Comments for Your Child:

folder where they keep all completed and/or published work from the week. Every other Friday, the fifth graders spread out on the floor and in the hallways, and review their folders. They arrange their work in order of importance to themselves as learners. The students write a letter to their parents about their work and what they have been studying over the past few weeks. Patti's students often refer to their Learning Logs while writing the letters. We've included an example of Patti's parent letter and response, as well as her Friday Folder Form.

Dear Parents,

This is your child's Friday Folder. The Friday Folder contains your child's school work and will come home every two weeks for your viewing pleasure. This folder also contains a letter to you from your child describing recent learnings and activities. The Friday Folder needs to be returned to school on Monday with work intact. The reasons for work coming back are threefold. First, some of the work is still in process. Second, your child will be taking time to reflect on his/her work and to set future learning goals. Finally, your child will also be selecting several pieces from the Friday Folder to keep in his/her classroom portfolio.

The classroom portfolio is an organizational tool for me, you, and your child to be able to view growth in all areas throughout the entire year. The portfolio will contain pieces that are significant to your child, either because the pieces showed improvement or because it was one they felt to be their "best." Each piece in the portfolio will be described and be accompanied by a self-reflection. Your child may take his/her portfolio home at the end of the year.

On the back of this letter is a place for you to comment every two weeks as you review the work with your child. Your observations and insights are important to me and your child!

Patricia Kamber

Over the weekend the parents can look through the student's work and make positive comments on the form provided. The Friday Folders show parents what their students have been learning and create a form of written dialogue between home and school.

Patti asks her students to bring their Friday Folder back to school by Monday. By Wednesday, most of the folders have trickled back, and the students spread out on the floor and sort their work. Students return unfinished stories or poems to their Writing Folders. Finished work can be placed in the filing cabinet or entered into their portfolios. Any piece they decide to include in their portfolios must be accompanied by written process notes, a description of the piece, and a self-reflection.

Self-Reflection

Here are some excerpts from the self-reflections that accompanied pieces in her students' portfolios. Note the depth of perceptions and the significant information that these comments reveal by the end of the year:

> I put this experiment in because it worked because this time I actually measured the chemicals. If you look at my November experiment you can see by the picture that I didn't measure and caused a minor explosion. I also recorded every step this time, and I didn't do that last time because I didn't really know what I was doing.

I like and dislike this poem. I like it because it has a lot of feeling and I think other kids that have to stay home by themselves at night could relate to it. I dislike this poem because I don't like to be reminded of staying home alone and it makes me mad. But for now, I will keep it in my portfolio because it's about an important idea. I don't want to put it into final draft yet. If ever.

This piece is important to me because it is the first time I ever had characters talk to each other. You know with quotation marks. I even went over their conversations in my sleep! The other extremely important thing about this paper is that I actually wanted to do a revision. Two revisions. And I liked the final copy. I've never done a revision on purpose before. I usually have just thought about it, and said I'll do better next time, but this time I wanted to fix it right away. I just didn't get tired of this piece like I have with other pieces. I also really liked the characters, Sam and Nicky, and wanted them to get to do something exciting. I didn't want them to have to be in a boring story. Sometimes I still think of other things Sam could do and how Nicky would save the situation. Maybe a sequel?

Peer Evaluation

Every other Wednesday, students share their portfolio with their peers. Patti gives them 5–10 minutes to look at one other person's portfolio, then write a positive comment to their classmate on a mailing label. The owner of the portfolio can choose where to keep these responses. When she calls, "portfolio pass," they pass the one they were examining on to the next person. Over time, the students have the opportunity to see each other's portfolios and come to know each other better. Here are some examples of supportive and perceptive comments they made to each other:

I think my favorite piece of yours would be a tie between your spaghetti invention and your acid rain invention. They are really creative. I would never in a million years have thought of making a ferris wheel to bring me my spaghetti or catch rain! Where and how did you get these great ideas?

Your poem on nature was beautiful! You used similes and they weren't even assigned. This poem is just, well, very descriptive. It changed since you last read it to me. You added the descriptions that you were telling me about, and I know that can be hard to do.

I read your poem about fears, and I wanted you to know that I am also very afraid of death.

Wow, you really write a lot of drafts for each of your stories! Doesn't your hand get tired? But your writing ends up so good! I really like your paper about, "When will there be a woman President?" Your ideas were in a really good order, and made sense to me, the writing didn't just go on and on you know like some stories do until you forget what the topic was, now what was I saying?

The second I looked at your portfolio, I mean in the very first three seconds, I could tell you like to write. I mean this portfolio is really thick and you use a lot of exclamation marks! I started to read your story on Dragons, and got so into it, that I didn't write you two comments, but I did finish the story, and it was excellent! But then you really like those Dragon Lance books don't you? You have 11 Dragon Lance books on your reading log! I really like your portfolio, it is also really colorful.

By visiting their portfolios on a regular basis, students reflect on their work and self-evaluation becomes a part of instruction. Portfolios become dynamic as students take pieces out and add others.

Portfolio Reviews

During the week, Patti meets individually with students for 5–10 minutes to discuss new entries in their portfolios and talk about what they are currently learning. She jots down anecdotal notes from their conversation and talks with students about goals. The child usually shares first, then Patti adds her observations. Once a month Patti takes the portfolios home, a few each night, and looks them over, writing each student a few comments about specific progress she has observed. On the next page is an example of Patti's notes from her Portfolio Review of one student.

Patti Kamber's philosophy and predictable schedule encourage students to view portfolios as dynamic and flexible. Portfolios can become what Donald Graves (1992) calls a "medium for reflection." Parents see the work from school and can easily communicate with Patti. This system is predictable and simple, yet provides regular opportunities to see students' portfolios, and come to know students very well as learners.

Sharing Portfolios

Since many parents work, Patti's class holds monthly Portfolio Evenings at school so families can come and celebrate their student's progress. She invites half of the students and their families one night, and the other half the next night. Families spread out around the room and look through their child's portfolio. Patti also sets aside one night at the end of the year as a final Portfolio Celebration. Since fifth grade is the last year at her elementary school, Patti's students and their parents look back fondly and a bit wistfully over the year, and take the portfolios home.

Several schools in South Australia have a similar method of communicating regularly with parents. The chapter called "Parents and Assessment" (Fryar, Johnston & Leaker, 1992) describes a program very similar to the one Patti Kamber has developed. *Portfolio Portraits* (Graves and Sunstein, 1992) also provides other examples of how teachers from first grade through college have implemented portfolios in a variety of ways. You'll need to develop a system that works for you. The more you read, visit other classrooms, and experiment with portfolios, the more confident you will become in developing portfolios as a way of celebrating growth and potential.

Portfolio Review for _____   Date **3/16/93**
Completed by **Mrs. Kamber**

Strengths

* Finished two challenging chapter books - independently!
  Tried a mystery and a biography - "even though I
  still love fantasy!"

* Writing coming easier (refer to journal, fiction pieces) using
  brainstorming lists - writing about "things I really care
  about."

Changes, Growth

- Included a math post test of a 95% "I studied and
  it worked!"

- Requested a speaking part in drama. "really really
  scarey, but I liked it alot!"

- Changed fiction piece to a new piece that "has just the right
  amount of details and the characters
Questions/concerns/comments   talk to each other."

"I am frustrated with my | - Added a more personal voice to his
speaking - kids don't | writing
always understand me" |

" I want to be a scientist and my portfolio doesn't show
          that yet!"
Goals

• to reflect "scientist" self in portfolio.

• talk to Ms. Fowler re speech hints

• read a non-fiction book - (maybe science + an
                              experiment as a
                              response activity)

TEACHERS' NOTEBOOKS

Since portfolios primarily contain student work and reflections, you will probably collect anecdotal notes and diagnostic information in your Teacher's Notebook. In each student's section, you may want to collect some of the following: anecdotal comments, running records, miscue analysis, checklists, or notes from parent conferences. Older students may want to keep attitude and interest surveys, and self-portraits in their own portfolios; however, you may want to keep those items for safekeeping with younger children.

The Organizational Checklist, developed by Cindy Ruptic, may provide a structure for deciding what assessment tools and techniques to use each month. Cindy's first version contains a list of 10 assessment tools that she uses to collect information about each student during the year. Some information might be kept in the students' portfolios. Cindy keeps most of the diagnostic information for her primary student in her Teacher's Notebook. She simply places a check in the blank rectangle when she collects the particular assessment information. For example, in September Cindy helped children fill out the Personal Inventory and asked students to draw a self-portrait. The next month she photocopied a writing sample from each student.

Cindy's second version on page 50 incorporates more components that she added as she became more comfortable using different assessment tools and techniques. We have included both forms and a blank version at the end of this section. You can list the tools you plan to use each month and create your own key. For instance, you might want to use a dot in the first box to indicate items that will be kept in your Teacher's Notebook, and an asterisk to show which items students will keep in their portfolios. Cindy's Organizational List is more comprehensive than the list of Portfolio Components, but they serve two distinct purposes. Patti and her students developed the list of Portfolio Components to guide their decisions about what to include in portfolios. Cindy's checklist was designed for teachers to use in organizing their whole assessment program. We've found that the Organizational Checklist can be used flexibly and helps keep you from becoming overwhelmed. It also provides a structure for collecting information about students on a systematic, rather than haphazard basis.

It's important to remember that your list will vary, depending on your district requirements, grade level, and your experience. Select the types of information to be collected. Be sure you are clear about your purpose for including each piece of information. Finally, develop a reasonable timeline for collecting information.

You will need to constantly reevaluate your system for collecting data. Like your students, you are continually growing and refining your work to reflect what you learn. The choice of items to include and your level of expectations will change as you experiment with various assessment tools. The goal should be to collect a variety of information from multiple sources in order to support all students as learners.

ORGANIZATIONAL CHECKLIST

Student _____ Year _____ Teacher(s) _____

ARTICLES TO BE COLLECTED:

ARTICLES TO BE COLLECTED:	SEPT	OCT	NOV	DEC	JAN	FEB	MAR	APR	MAY	JUNE
Personal Inventory										
* Self Portrait										
• Writing Sample/Fix-it										
Reading Conference Form(s)/Notes										
Taped Reading										
• Progress Reports										
* Reading and Writing Continuums										
* Reading Log										
• Thematic (Content Area) Project(s)										
* Student Selected Writing Samples										

Dates of entries:

ADDITIONAL (OPTIONAL) CONTENTS:

* From Student's Portfolio
• For Learning Profile

ORGANIZATIONAL CHECKLIST   Student _____   Year _____   Teacher(s) _____

ARTICLES TO BE COLLECTED:	SEPT	OCT	NOV	DEC	JAN	FEB	MAR	APR	MAY	JUNE
Initial Screening (letters, sounds, words)										
Concepts About Print										
Personal Inventory										
* Self Portrait/Pen Portrait										
High Frequency Words										
Reading Conference Form(s)/Notes										
Taped Reading										
• Writing Sample/"Fix-It"										
Spelling 10 Words										
Reading/Writing Questionnaire										
• Progress Reports										
• Reading and Writing Continuums										
Three-Way Conference Records										
* Reading Log										
* Reading Projects										
* Thematic (Content Area) Project(s)										
• Primary Math Checklist										
* Student Selected Writing Samples										
* Student Self-Evaluation										

ADDITIONAL (OPTIONAL) CONTENTS:	Dates of entries:					
* Math Projects						
* Additional Thematic Project(s)						
* Photographs						
* Artwork						
* Additional Written Pieces						
Teacher Observations/Anecdotal Records						
Parent Questionnaires						
Parent Observations						

* From Student's Portfolio
• Required for District Learning Profile Project

ORGANIZATIONAL CHECKLIST

Student _____ Year _____ Teacher(s) _____

ARTICLES TO BE COLLECTED:

	SEPT	OCT	NOV	DEC	JAN	FEB	MAR	APR	MAY	JUNE

ADDITIONAL(OPTIONAL) CONTENTS:

Dates of entries:

	SEPT	OCT	NOV	DEC	JAN	FEB	MAR	APR	MAY	JUNE

CHAPTER FIVE

Observing Students

One of the delights of teaching is watching young children grow. Sometimes it seems a child has become fluent at writing almost overnight. Once in a while we see the light bulb go on as a child leaps from decoding into the "aha" that comes with "really reading." We can learn so much by listening to children argue about why dinosaurs became extinct or discuss favorite books. One way to capture the learning steps and poignant moments that occur in the classroom is to capture these anecdotes in writing.

ANECDOTAL RECORDS

Anecdotal records are brief written notes based on observations of students. "It's November and Randy still cries when his mother leaves him at school." "Gloria will be out another week with strep throat." "Garret shared his poem at Author's Chair today. He says it's the first poem he's ever written." Many teachers keep notes like these on bits of paper or "Post-it" notes, but never really know what to do with this writing. Systematic anecdotal records help teachers document student behavior and learning. Anecdotal records can also capture the personal insights and vignettes that make teaching so rewarding. For some teachers, the use of anecdotal records can be a first step toward authentic assessment.

Why Use Anecdotal Records?

As Marie Clay says, "Educators have done a great deal of systematic testing and relatively little systematic observation of learning" (Clay, 1993, p. 7). The use of anecdotal records enables teachers to become what Yetta Goodman (1985) calls "kidwatchers" and better listeners. Keeping anecdotal notes also helps us get to know individual students. Our observations can then help us develop instruction to meet each child's needs. Written records provide information that can be used to:

- evaluate students' learning
- help make instructional decisions for individual students
- help make instructional decisions for the whole class
- determine which students need extra assistance
- look for patterns in student behavior
- provide documentation for parents and staff
- evaluate your own teaching

You will find that the more you keep anecdotal records, the more you will notice about your students and the easier it will be to recognize patterns of student growth.

Anecdotal records readjust the teacher's vision of who and where the student is and sharpens teachers' insight into how each student travels along his or her own path to learning. Only when we look as if with a magnifying glass can we see and hear individual and idiosyncratic child-based standards of growth, accomplishment, and failure. (Matthews, 1992, p. 169)

What Kind of Information Do You Record?

It's important that you decide your purpose for taking anecdotal notes and whether you will keep your notes private or share them with others. Either way, you should be careful to record observations rather than making judgments. For instance, "Jessica often leans her head on her desk and closes her eyes during the day" is more accurate than "Jessica needs more sleep," which is an assumption that may or may not be true. You can always add your opinion or question to your observations: "Enrico most often seems to play alone at recess. I wonder why?" Although you may intend to keep your notes private, there is always a chance someone else may read something you've written.

It's helpful to record information in different contexts, such as at recess, during quiet reading time, and during literature circles. You may want to record some of the following information:

- specific behaviors in different contexts
- choices of activities
- choices of friends
- skills/strategies the student uses
- notes to yourself about ways to support learning
- records of conversations
- records of skills/strategies taught
- breakthroughs
- funny comments

It's also helpful to develop criteria to focus on while taking anecdotal records during specific times. For instance, during literature circles, you may want to look for the following: Are the students developing insights about the setting? Are they sharing emotional and personal reactions to the book? Are they considering and respecting the opinions of others? If you find yourself writing too many notes, you might want to develop a simple checklist of four or five main focus questions. These might change from week to week.

Three important things to remember are: Date Everything! Be Specific! Be Brief! You shouldn't spend more than a minute or two jotting down notes about a child. Lengthy descriptions aren't necessary.

How Do You Get Started?

One way to begin using anecdotal records is to focus on only one context or content area. For instance, you may want to keep notes only during writing workshop or during silent reading time. Another way to begin is to start with one or two students a day or a small group of four or five students for one week. Some teachers write down comments as they talk with students, while others prefer to step aside afterwards and jot down notes. Students will be curious about what you are writing. We've found it helpful to explain that you're jotting down things you want to remember and show them a few examples.

The best time to observe children is when they are busy! Keep your clipboard handy and jot down a few notes every day during writer's workshop, quiet reading, or literature circles. Regie Routman's section in *Invitations: Changing as Teachers and Learners K–12* (1991, pp. 389–

317) on anecdotal records is particularly helpful. She cautions that some teachers take several years before they are comfortable with this form of ongoing assessment. "As you begin to make taking anecdotal records a part of your teaching, eventually, the task will no longer seem like an extra incumbrance, and you will feel as though you know your students a lot better" (p. 317).

ORGANIZING ANECDOTAL RECORDS

We have found six effective methods for using anecdotal records, although there are probably many more. Keeping anecdotal records must be simple or you won't keep it up. If you have to copy notes over into a notebook, they will often get buried on your desk. You need a simple system for storing information.

Notebook: Many teachers keep a three-ring binder with a section for every student. It helps to have tabs with the students' names so you can locate each child's section quickly. Each child's section may contain several pages, one for each subject area. You could also include other assessment forms such as the Reading Conference Record or Interest Survey in the same notebook. The advantage of a notebook is that everything is in one place.

Folders: Other teachers prefer having a separate notebook or folder for different subjects, such as one for writing workshop and one for literature circles. You may also want to have a Personal Folder or Notebook with emergency numbers, records of conversations you've had with parents, and confidential information. The nice thing about a folder is that you can focus on one area at a time and at conference time transfer your pages into your notebook. A folder is also more portable.

File Cards: It's preferable to use 5 × 8 inch cards so that you have enough room to write information. You can keep a card for each child on a ring and file it when the card is full. Cards can be stored in a file box or layered on a file folder like a flip chart with each child's name showing (see photograph). You may want to have one flip chart for each subject area such as writing, reading, and content areas.

Computer: Teachers with expertise in technology who have access to a desk-top or lap-top computer in the classroom may wish to keep anecdotal records on a disk. If a word processing program is kept active throughout the day, you can record comments immediately. Using "cut and paste" editing functions, you can transfer the comments to individual student files. You then can use these comments to produce a "pen portrait" or narrative comments for conferences or cumulative records. Programs that integrate word processing, spreadsheets, and databases allow an even greater range of capabilities for sorting and classifying information to make reports.

"Post-it" Notes: "Post-it" notes are a wonderful invention for teachers! You can tuck a pad in your pocket and later transfer your notes to individual pages in your Teacher's Notebook or onto file cards. The advantage of using "Post-it" notes is that they are easy to carry and can be moved; the disadvantage is that they lose their stickiness after a while. We've provided a form for keeping anecdotal records using "Post-it" notes at the end of this chapter.

Mailing Labels: The same process can be used with sheets of mailing labels. They work well because they don't blow off and they stick better; however, they can only be moved once.

Sheets of blank mailing labels are available that can be run through a copy machine. You can photocopy several pages of mailing labels with the names of your students. You can write anecdotal comments on the mailing labels, then transfer the labels to your Notebook, Folder, or File Cards.

You'll probably end up combining several of these techniques, perhaps using "Post-it" notes and a notebook or mailing labels and folders. Many teachers like to have a clipboard tucked away in a handy place in the classroom. Color-coded forms and notebook dividers with tabs appeal to those who love organization. Whatever system you start with, it will probably change as you experiment with what works best for you and your particular style. Some teachers "keep everything in their head"; however, with 20–30 students, it's very difficult to recall specific incidents, conversations, poignant remarks, and funny stories. Anecdotal notes are intended to be for you, but you may wish to summarize the information on progress reports, at staffings, or at parent conferences. Using anecdotal notes will help you to be specific and accurate. In addition, the process of keeping and reviewing anecdotal records can give you valuable information about your teaching. For example, there may be one or two students for whom you have no notes. If you weren't taking anecdotal notes, you might never realize how much that child was "invisible."

The Anecdotal Record Form

We've provided a blank form at the end of this section with little blocks the size of small "Post-it" notes. If you write in all the names of your students, you can run off several copies of the form, then place blank sticky notes below each name. You'll then have a note for each student.

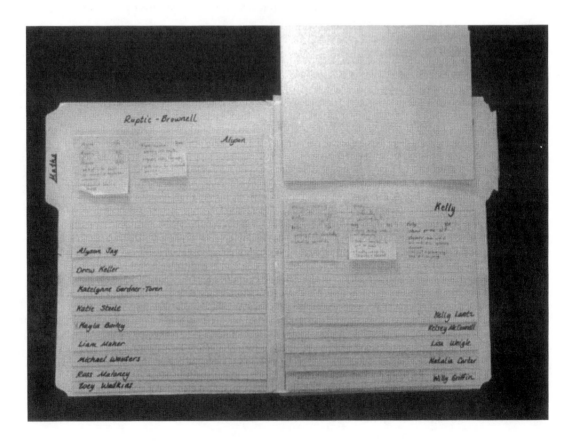

ANECDOTAL RECORDS for _____

If you make more than one observation about a student, you can simply stack the sticky notes under his/her name. We've found this organized method of keeping anecdotal notes helps us observe and record information about every child. You could also use this form periodically for what Nancie Atwell (1987) termed a "status-of-the-class" chart for any particular area of the curriculum or for recording titles of books primary students choose for quiet reading time.

The next page shows how Cindy uses a blank page for "Post-it" notes in her Teacher's Notebook for anecdotal comments about the students in her class. Once the page of "Post-it" notes for the whole class is full, she moves the "Post-it" notes to children's individual pages. Once the page is full, Cindy photocopies the individual page and throws away all the sticky notes. She has discovered that yellow "Post-it" notes photocopy better than other colors.

The last version of form on page 60 show a sample of Cindy's comments about one child, arranged in chronological order. Cindy uses these comments when she writes narrative comments on the progress report and refers to her anecdotal notes during parent conferences.

From Anecdotal Notes to Checklists

Many teachers find that they are recording the same comments repeatedly for certain content areas. This lack of efficiency is one of the reasons we started working on this book! We wanted to take common comments and make checklists for specific activities, such as writer's workshop and literature circles. Although we've provided a great number of forms in this book, we hope you'll modify and adapt them to suit your own needs. The forms you will find most useful are the ones you've developed or adapted. As Edward Chittenden (1991) said, "One person's favorite rating sheet is another's income tax form" (p. 25). In the next chapter, we'll introduce specific tools for assessing the growth of emergent readers and writers.

Alice	Brad	David	Dylan
1/19 Beginning to read more difficult (Nate the Great) chapter books competently w/ minimal help... hard work, but can do it!	1/11 Talked about getting off the video game words and stretching yourself me exasperated about his being stuck in the mire of copying w/Harry Took it well – contrite, agreed w/me, made commitment to do more.	1/15 Needing to go to the bathroom a lot. He also noticed this – said he would speak to his parents	1/15 Serious about taking responsibility for his own learning. Stayed in at recess to finish Only took 5 minutes Well done

Elizabeth	Harry	Jeri	Kathleen
1/12 Off the wall all AM! Popping up and down, interrupting, off-task, noises and other sounds, repeated redirections necessary ~respectful behavior discussed	1/17 Writing story about "Baseball Diamond Mystery" w/Andy – Prominent swastichas ⌗ all over it and drawing of what looks like Hitler... nothing said yet, but watching this.	1/8 W/Kleenex reading Annie Sullivan "This is sad" "Do any more people die?" Talked about whether to continue – it's okay to cry/feel sad w/books	1/11 Finished "Kathleen Wore Her..." book Nudged to correct the few misspelled words – 1st time

Lawrence	Mandy	Michael	Nancy
	1/12 Really pleased First day to bring lunch packed at home rather than buying school lunch. "I made it myself!"	1/17 Making a book about fishing trip w/ lift-up flaps showing fish + names of them	

Paul	Randy	Ricky	Susan
1/15 Went to Lawrence's on the bus, but Mom still came by at the end of the day... to check on him?	1/19 On time every day this week... maybe we've licked the tardiness problem?		1/11 Very helpful getting Tory caught up after long illness. Good "teacher"; shows how to, then does own work side-by-side ready to assist "student".

Thomas	Tory	Vince	Zoey
			1/13 Shocked and wanted to share with me what she was reading about M.L. King jr.

12/17 Had to go home w/mom; crying right at 8:45 — called her to take her home — "big fight" Mom/Dad re: work	12/18 Home again at 8:45 Back at 9:30 to "help do things for others" after calming down	1/4 Crying again during "Attendance" job... Difficult goodbye w/Mo. Stress connected w/ Dad's lay-off and holidays	1/7 Tearless, normal start Even Able to take redirects at writing (off-talk) calmly
1/11 Very helpful getting Tory caught up after long illness. Good "teacher" shows how t. then does own work side-by-side ready to assist "student"	1/21 Having trouble finishing <u>Sacajawea</u> She can read it, but it is a real challenge and seems not to hold her interest. Rdg level/ maturity level issue?	2/1 "I'm not sure I want to do these tubs again" Offered options: Latin Cubes ★ Estimating ! recording w/ >< = ★ chose this	2/2 Working on chapter book of her own autobiography — 4 chapters so far
2/12 Good compromising in problem solving activity w/ Theo, Trent and Alanna	3/1 Author's Circle for her autobiography; planning to use comments/questions for revision		

CHAPTER SIX

Observing Emergent Writers and Readers

Jerry shares his story about dinosaurs at Author's Chair, written in invented spelling that only he can read. Sabrina has memorized *The Napping House* (Wood, 1984), which she "reads" to a group of friends on the rug. Mark and Carmen use the notepad in the home center as they take orders while they "play restaurant." These children are in a kindergarten classroom that successfully launches children into reading, writing, and the world of school. Teachers can assess these children's developing competence with written language through observations, collecting samples, and talking with these young readers and writers.

Pencil and paper tests simply cannot capture young children's developing understanding of oral and written language, and their growing concepts about the world around them. Primary teachers must be able to observe and evaluate their young children's emerging competencies in order to support a child's next steps. The use of anecdotal records described in the last chapter is one way to assess children. In addition, it's important to become aware of the patterns of young children's writing and reading development.

We want to stress here that the forms we are including in this chapter are designed to help you gather information about your young readers and writers. The more you learn, the more you can build upon each child's growing concepts about language and literacy. For instance, the information from the Letter Recognition/Sound Identification form can help you understand Christie's invented spelling strategies. That information can help you plan experiences with predictable texts before launching into decoding. The results *should not* be interpreted as meaning you need to drill Christie on letter sounds! Your instruction should be child-centered and responsive; the assessment tools merely provide clues about each child's strengths and needs. In this chapter we will describe several types of forms specifically designed for assessing children's early explorations as writers and readers.

EMERGENT WRITING AND READING

Researchers in the field of emergent literacy (Hall, 1987; Harste, Woodward & Burke, 1984; Morrow, 1989; Newkirk, 1989; Teale & Sulzby, 1986) have documented how writing and reading develop almost from birth. The term *emergent literacy* first was used by Marie Clay in her doctoral dissertation in 1966 and describes children's developmental process of becoming literate.

Our job as teachers is to build upon the concepts about oral and written language that children bring to school and create an environment where children can experiment with language.

Dorothy Strickland and Lesley Morrow's book, *Emerging Literacy: Young Children Learn to Read and Write* (1989) provides a good review of current research in this area, as well as some helpful suggestions for teaching young children. Knowledge of the development of children's concepts about print and emergent literacy provides a framework for making observations. Understanding of oral and written language development can help you know what to look for and become more confident about the patterns of literacy acquisition. The forms that we've created help document early writing and reading development. We want to be able to show parents and other teachers how children progress from scribbling, to writing random strings of letters, to using invented spelling. We also want to note children's increasing competence as readers.

Why Use Emergent Writing and Reading Forms?

When you date specific literacy behaviors on the forms, you can begin to see patterns of literacy development that reflect each child's growth over time. By filling out these forms, you'll be taking the time to reflect on each child's growing competency as a writer and reader. In addition, by placing the whole class on one page, you can glimpse the range of literacy development for the class as a whole. The information from the class profile can help you plan how to support children's next steps in writing and reading.

You can also use the information about your class to explain the stages of literacy development to parents. The data is helpful for those parents who are concerned about "how their child compares to other students." Showing the wide range of development among students can sometimes help parents see that learning to read and write are natural developmental processes. At parent conferences, you can then highlight both individual growth and the range of development for children of a particular age. Finally, whole-class profiles of literacy development can provide useful long-term information at grade level, building, and district levels.

Emergent Writing and Reading Development Forms

The Emergent Writing and Reading Development forms on the following pages help teachers and parents see a child's progress over time. We've included an actual sample from Roz Duthie, the kindergarten teacher who developed these forms. List the names of your students in the left column on the reading and writing forms. Keep the form on a clipboard, so you can simply place the date (month and year) by the stage of development for each child. Some teachers find it easier to concentrate on a few children each day. You can examine their writing samples, observe them during writing time, and talk with children individually. You may wish to periodically review writing samples from the whole class. When you review samples each term after conferring with students, you can also update the information on the forms.

Some teachers meet with children individually for reading conferences. Others may want to make notes throughout the day as children interact with books. For instance, you may wish to record a child's degree of participation during story time or while sharing Big Books with the class.

We've found that discussions with students often reveal helpful information about a child's understanding of the writing and reading processes, and products. Throughout the day you can write anecdotal notes about a child's reading and writing on "Post-it" notes. Later, you can transfer the information to your Teacher's Notebook or onto the reading and writing development forms. The terminology and stages of reading and writing development match the ones used on the continuums described in Chapter 13.

EMERGENT READING DEVELOPMENT

NAME	PRECONVENTIONAL • Book awareness • Letter names • Responds to stories • Chooses favorites • Interest in environmental print	EMERGENT • Pretends to read • Some letter sounds • Plays w/words/rhymes • Memorizes books • Pictures=story	DEVELOPING • Reads predictable books • Sees self as a reader • Concept of words • Recognizes simple words • Print+pictures=story • Retells main idea	BEGINNING • Reads early reader books • Expands word recognition • Develops sense of story • Begins to read silently • Uses phonics and some other strategies	EXPANDING • Easy chapter books • Uses varied strategies • Reads silently • Increased fluency and expression • Retells stories
1					
2					
3					
4					
5					
6					
7					
8					
9					
10					
11					
12					
13					
14					
15					
16					
17					
18					
19					
20					
21					
22					
23					
24					
25					

EMERGENT WRITING DEVELOPMENT

NAME	PRECONVENTIONAL •Scribbling •Pictures=meaning •Pictures w/"words" •Random letters •Tells about writing BMTYZ=WORD	EMERGENT •Copies names/words •Pictures+print •Mainly upper case •Beginning/ending consonants •Pretend reads writing WD or YD=WORD	DEVELOPING •Directional conventions •Upper & lower case •Uses some spacing •Some letters based on sounds •Reads own writing WRD=WORD	BEGINNING •Others can read •Complete thoughts •Punctuation experiments •Inventive spelling •Some words spelled correctly WERD=WORD	EXPANDING •Awareness of spelling patterns/rules •Capitals/periods •Beginning/middle/end •Add-on revision •Begins to write fluently WORD=WORD
1 Karley A.	9/92	1/93 →			
2 Mackenzie B.	9/92 1/93	→			
3 Paul B.	9/92 →	1/93			
4 Zach C.	9/92	1/93			
5 Lucas C.	9/92 1/93				
6 Win D.		9/92	1/93		
7 William D.	9/92 1/93				
8 Tiffany E.			11/92	2/93	
9 Clayton H.	11/92 →	12/92			
10 Nicole H.			1/93		
11 Julie H.	9/92 2/93				
12 Molly J.	9/92 1/93				
13 Kirstin L.		9/92	2/93		
14 Michelle M.		9/92		2/93	
15 J.J. M.	9/92/2/93 No growth!				
16 Robbie O.	9/92				
17 Adrian S.			2/93		
18 Ryan S.	9/92	2/93 →			
19 Patrick S.	9/92	2/93			
20 Alex W.	9/92	2/93 w/help			
21					
22					
23					
24					
25					

EMERGENT WRITING DEVELOPMENT

NAME	PRECONVENTIONAL	EMERGENT	DEVELOPING	BEGINNING	EXPANDING
	•Scribbling •Pictures=meaning •Pictures w/"words" •Random letters •Tells about writing BMTYZ=WORD	•Copies names/words •Pictures+print •Mainly upper case •Beginning/ending consonants •Pretend reads writing WD or YD=WORD	•Directional conventions •Upper & lower case •Uses some spacing •Some letters based on sounds •Reads own writing WRD=WORD	•Others can read •Complete thoughts •Punctuation experiment •Inventive spelling •Some words spelled correctly WERD=WORD	•Awareness of spelling patterns/rules •Capitals/periods •Beginning/middle/end •Add-on revision •Begins to write fluently WORD=WORD
1					
2					
3					
4					
5					
6					
7					
8					
9					
10					
11					
12					
13					
14					
15					
16					
17					
18					
19					
20					
21					
22					
23					
24					
25					

WRITING WORDS

You can learn a great deal about young writers by observing them at work. For instance, Tanya prints neatly, using all upper-case letters, and leaves spaces between her words. She seems to have memorized several sight words and relies on "sounding out" most other words. Tanya's journal entries usually consist of three- or four-word phrases. Taking anecdotal notes and using some of the forms described in this chapter can help paint a picture of Tanya as a writer.

Marie Clay (1993) describes a very simple assessment technique in which you simply ask children to write all the words they know in ten minutes, beginning with their name. Some children may only write part of their name or a word or two, while others can write as many as forty words. Clay's book provides specific directions for scoring, based on tests of large numbers of children. You may simply want to use this technique two or three times a year in order to document growth. As you collect the data over a few years, you will be better able to note trends for your particular grade level and population. Since no materials are needed other than a watch, pencil, and paper, we have described the procedure, but not included any forms for this technique.

READING WORDS

Information about a child's growing recognition of sight words can easily be assessed by parent helpers or aides. Two or three times a year, an adult can ask children to read from a list of Dolch words to note developing reading skills. The adults can highlight words the child reads correctly by using a different color pen for each trimester. For instance, each fall, Randi Ivancich highlights the words the child recognizes in yellow. She uses a green highlighter in the winter and a pink one in the spring. Randi finds the use of different colors helps parents and students visually see each child's growth in reading. She *does not* explicitly teach these words; the record merely provides a graphic demonstration of how many words and strategies young children absorb naturally in a literature-based classroom.

PRIMARY INITIAL SCREENING FORM

Many of you who teach kindergarten or first grade already use a screening tool such as Marie Clay's Letter Identification or Concepts About Print tests. Her recent book, *An Observational Survey of Early Literacy Achievement* (1993), provides detailed descriptions on administering and scoring these tools.

You probably screen children less formally to test their knowledge of color names, letter names and sounds, and ability to count. Susan Fowler piloted the Primary Initial Screening form on Bainbridge Island for several years. Each fall all first grade teachers now use this tool to screen students. Each child is tested individually. You may wish to calculate scores as a percentage. Students whose scores fall below a certain range can then be further tested individually by a reading specialist or Chapter I teacher. This form meets with federal guidelines for Chapter I and has proven a valid tool for red-flagging children they want to observe more closely.

Note that the lower-case alphabet contains both kinds of type styles for the letters a, g, and l. Susan also carefully separated confusing letters, such as b and d. The word recognition section progresses from sight words to simple words that children can decode phonetically.

The Primary Intital Screening form on the next page is fairly self-explanatory. We've made two pages that contain all the letters, numbers, and words from the form in large print. Again, we want to stress that this tool is less authentic than many others in this section. The results

PRIMARY INITIAL SCREENING

Student's Name_____ Grade:_____ Screener: _____ Date:_____

Alphabet Identification:

B K P T V Z D J C R O H A U G I Q E W F M X N S L Y

a g l b k p t v z d j c r o h a u g i q e w f m x n s l y

Sound-Letter Association:

B K P T V Z D J C R O H A U G I Q E W F M X N S L Y

Number Identification: 3 7 8 1 4 2 5 9 6 10 13 17 18 11 14 12 15 19 16 20

Counting: How far can student count without error?   _____

Color Identification: red   yellow   blue   green   orange   purple   white   black

Word Identification: go   me   the   yes   trip   stop   came   time   cat   tree   dog   hat   bug

Observations/Comments:

PRIMARY INITIAL SCREENING

Student's Name_____ Grade: _____ Screener: _____ Date:_____

Alphabet Identification:

B K P T V Z D J C R O H A U G I Q E W F M X N S L Y

a g l b k p t v z d j c r o h a u g i q e w f m x n s l y

Sound-Letter Association:

B K P T V Z D J C R O H A U G I Q E W F M X N S L Y

Number Identification: 3 7 8 1 4 2 5 9 6 10 13 17 18 11 14 12 15 19 16 20

Counting: How far can student count without error?   _____

Color Identification: red   yellow   blue   green   orange   purple   white   black

Word Identification: go   me   the   yes   trip   stop   came   time   cat   tree   dog   hat   bug

Observations/Comments:

C	E	a	d	i	l
J	Q	Y	z	g	s
D	I	L	v	u	n
Z	G	S	t	a	x
V	U	N	p	h	m
T	A	X	k	o	f
P	H	M	b	r	w
K	O	F	l	c	e
B	R	W	g	j	q

9	5	4	1	8	7	3
15	12	11	18	17	13	10
		2	14			19	16

orange green blue red me go

purple black stop cat yes the

yellow white trip hat bug dog

came time tree

would need to be substantiated by observing children's reading and writing processes, and examining their work. We would hope that teachers would not "teach" the letters a child doesn't know in isolation, but would continue to surround the child with many types of print and talk about letters and sounds in the natural context of reading and writing.

LETTER RECOGNITION/SOUND ASSOCIATION FORM

This form is helpful for teachers who work with beginning readers and writers. You can use the letter recognition form with emergent readers to determine their developing concepts about print. Kindergarten and first grade teachers quickly become masters at reading invented spelling, and develop an intuitive sense for the stages of emergent reading and writing. One kindergarten teacher, Roz Duthie, developed what she's nicknamed the "ED-DUH" form based on her observations about a specific developmental stage of writing and reading.

Research shows that a child's ability to recognize letters in print and understand the concept of corresponding sounds, directly correlates with the child's emergent reading and writing development. The predominant tradition in our culture is to teach children the names of letters before teaching them the sounds the letters represent. Young children acquiring language are very auditory learners and are usually introduced to letter names through the alphabet song. Consequently, before children recognize the letters visually, they already know or can sing the letter names. It is at home and preschool, as well as through T.V. and environmental print that children learn to connect the letter name with the correct symbol.

Learning the sounds letters make is a challenging task in English! Children recognize the letter "B" before they learn that the letter "B" makes a "buh" sound. This connection is simple for seven other consonants; these are the letters children learn most easily: B, D, J, K, P, T, V, and Z. These rather straightforward consonants appear on the top row of this form.

Other letter sounds are more difficult for children to acquire. Some letters, such as vowels, represent several sounds. Several consonants also have more than one initial sound, like "G," which can be soft ("juh" as in giraffe) or hard ("guh" as in gun). Then there are the tricky letters with names that end with the sound they represent or just don't sound much like the letter they represent. For example, when we say the letter "R," the sound we make is "ahr." Yet the initial "R" sound is actually the last sound children hear when they say "R" ("rrrr"). The natural tendency of a child trying to decode this challenging alphabet and associated sounds is to apply the rule that seemed at first to fit all letters. If "B says buh," shouldn't "R say ah"? Many emergent readers will tell you that it does. They will also tell you that the sound for "H" is "ay," rather than the quietly breathy "huh" that we use for words beginning with "H." Many of these more challenging letter sounds appear in the second row of the Letter Identification/Sound Recognition Form.

The remaining nine letters consistently present similar problems for young learners and form a distinct group. The letters F, L, M, N, and S present a collective hurdle for emergent readers and writers. A child's inability to link these letters with their respective sounds places the child in a very distinct phase of development. Almost all children seem to pass through this phase before they can name the initial sounds of the entire alphabet. These five letters all begin with the sound "eh." For instance, "F" is "ehf" and "L" is "ehl." The decoding strategy children try with "B" and "D" simply doesn't work with these five letters.

Until children understand that the sounds represented by the letters most often do not directly correlate to the initial sounds we hear when we say the name of the letters, they continue to apply the simple rule that worked with "B" and "D." Children at this stage will say that "S" makes the sound "eh" and so do F, L, M, and N. They say "eh" because that's the sound the child first hears when saying the names of these letters. (Actually, if we can get them to hear the *last* sound the "eh" letters make, they can make another decoding connection.)

LETTER RECOGNITION/SOUND ASSOCIATION

Name_____   Teacher_____   Date_____

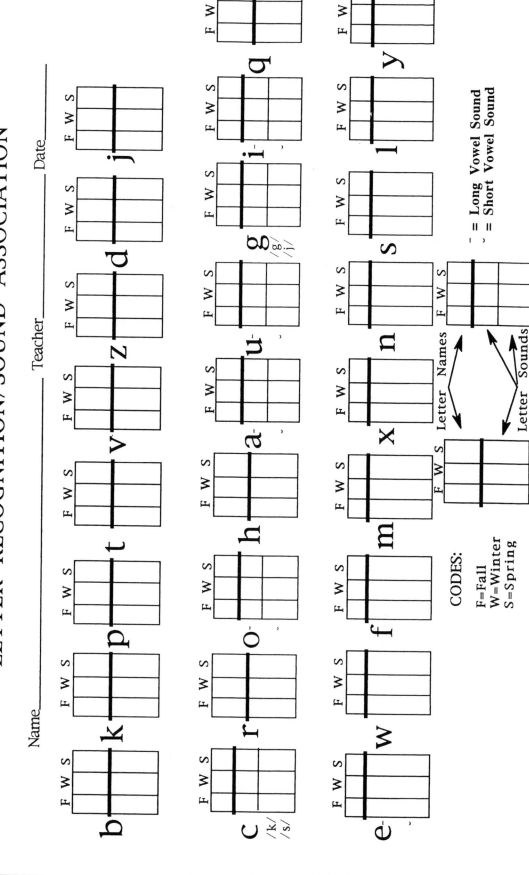

CODES:

F=Fall
W=Winter
S=Spring

Letter Names

Letter Sounds

‾ = Long Vowel Sound
˘ = Short Vowel Sound

LETTER RECOGNITION/SOUND ASSOCIATION

Name _____ Teacher _____ Date _____

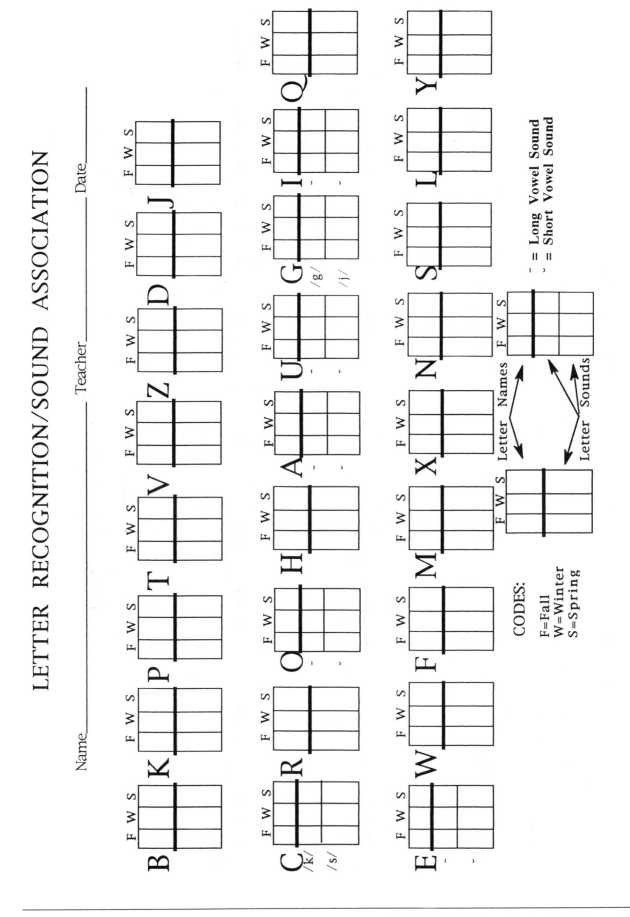

CODES:

F=Fall
W=Winter
S=Spring

= Long Vowel Sound
= Short Vowel Sound

Letter Names

Letter Sounds

When it comes to learning the short sound for the vowel, "E," "eh" becomes doubly confusing.

The two remaining letters, "W" and "Y" present an additional challenge. There is absolutely no connection between the sound of the name "double yoo" and the sound the letter "W" conveys in print. Children stuck on the sounds of the "eh" letters will similarly describe the sound of "W" as "duh." To their way of thinking, the sound for "Y" becomes "wuh."

Roz found that a great majority of children reach this "eh" (for F, L, M, N, S) and "duh" (for W) stage after learning all the alphabet letter names and some of the sounds. Children will stay in this phase until they realize there is no one rule that will apply to learning letter sounds (and that, indeed, some of them make no sense at all). Children in the "EH-DUH" phase of sound acquisition are usually not quite ready to read on their own. At this stage, the words they attempt to write independently most likely consist of only beginning and ending consonants. They are truly "emergent" readers and writers, and will move on to the next phase of reading and writing when they acquire the remainder of the letter sounds.

By using the Letter Recognition/Sound Association form on the next page, divided in this way by the types of letters, Roz found she could easily determine a child's understanding of letter and sound correlations. The information will allow you to analyze a child's developmental strategies and what you can next expect in terms of writing and decoding skills. The information can also help you direct and encourage individual learning appropriate to the skill level of each child. This form uses capital letters since those are the letters children first learn to recognize and write.

Rather than teaching these "missing sounds" in isolation, you can encourage children to notice environmental print and the names of children in the classroom, and experiment with word patterns and written language. Current research on early reading shows that children focus as much on initial phonemes, called the "onset," and the first syllable, called the "rime" (Adams, 1990). These psychological units of sound can best be supported by exposure to print and play with words, such as rhyming. The focus of reading should always be on enjoyment and making meaning, rather than on letters and sounds in isolation.

ADDITIONAL INFORMATION

For many children in the early stages of literacy development, progress in writing appears to precede their development in reading. Some children may find that the more active nature of writing is more appealing, while others may be fascinated by the fact that they can write about people and things that matter in their lives. The avenue into literacy through writing is a powerful option for many children. This may be particularly true when children are encouraged to write daily, even in kindergarten.

Two books that we've found particularly helpful as we designed assessment and evaluation tools for kindergarten are *Joyful Learning: A Whole Language Kindergarten* (Fisher, 1991), and *Teaching Kindergarten: A Developmental Approach* (Walmsley, Camp & Walmsley, 1992). Three practical books on assessing and writing in first grade are: *Managing Literacy Assessment with Young Learners* (Weeks and Leaker, 1991), *The Author's Chair and Beyond* (Karelitz, 1993), and *. . . And with a Light Touch* (Avery 1993).

It's also worth noting that for young children, drawing and writing are often intertwined. Art can play an important part in classrooms of older students as well. Writing and drawing are both symbol systems. You can learn a great deal by examining children's growth as artists, as well as writers. You may wish to collect samples of children's artwork in addition to their writing samples. Three helpful books that examine children's artistic development are *Authors of Pictures, Draughtsmen of Words* (Hubbard, 1989), *First Drawings: Genesis of Visual Thinking* (Fein, 1993), and *Heidi's Horse* (Fein, 1993). In *Heidi's Horse*, Sylvia Fein has presented 250 drawings that document the development in children's drawings between the ages of two and seventeen. Ruth Hubbard posits,

> Drawing is not just for children who can't yet write fluently, and creating pictures is not just part of rehearsal for real writing. Images *at any age* are part of the serious business of making meaning—partners with words for communicating our inner designs. (p. 157)

Children's drawings can reflect their interests, illuminate the themes in their lives, and reveal their increasing proficiency and confidence as artists. You can also gain valuable insights into your students' views of drawing and writing through individual conferences, observations, and interviews. In the next two chapters, we'll discuss further ways to assess children's growth in writing and reading.

CHAPTER SEVEN

Observing Writing Growth

In many ways observing growth in writing is much easier than in reading since there is a written product. You can glean a great deal of information by observing children as they write, as well as from interviews and surveys. In this chapter we will briefly review a process approach to teaching writing. If this information is new to you, we would urge you to read the inspiring books by Donald Graves (1983), Lucy Calkins (1986), and Nancie Atwell (1987) described in the section on Getting Started in Chapter 3. For most of us, our movement toward whole language began with changes in how we taught writing.

In Chapter 6, we described the stages of emergent writing and provided several forms documenting the beginning stages of writing development. Here we will provide a few forms that we have developed for assessing more fluent writers' process and mechanics.

PROCESS WRITING

In his landmark book, *Writing: Teachers and Children at Work* (1983), Donald Graves posited that children come to school ready to write. Our job is to nurture that positive attitude, to encourage risk-taking, and to demonstrate the strategies that good writers employ as they compose. Donald Graves and Lucy Calkins (1986) first described the predictable structure of a writing workshop. Teachers usually begin with a "mini-lesson" on a particular topic or strategy. Students then have blocks of time every day to write about topics of their own choosing. Children can confer with teachers and share their writing with each other. Teachers write alongside their students and share their excitement about the power of writing. Assessment is an integral part of writer's workshop. As students write, the teacher can move around the room observing and talking with students. This is the perfect time for a teacher to take anecdotal notes as described in Chapter 5.

Traditionally, teachers assigned a writing topic at the beginning of the week. Students handed in their papers on Friday, with little help during the composition process. As Lucy Calkins (1986) says, writing was assigned rather than taught. In a workshop approach, writing is viewed as an ongoing process that involves prewriting, drafting, revising, editing, and sometimes publishing a variety of pieces. Teachers give demonstration lessons, confer with students, model writing strategies, and share their own writing. Many excellent books provide more information on the specifics of this approach. Since our assessment forms are based on a process approach to teaching writing, however, we wanted to explain these components briefly.

WRITING FOLDER FORMS

The forms on the next set of pages are the Writing Folder Forms described in Chapter 3. On the first form, students can record possible topics for writing. Lucy Calkins describes how teachers can model topic selection the first day of writing workshop. Students can add to their topic list throughout the year.

On the next form, writers can list the titles of pieces they've written. We've purposely used the term "pieces" to emphasize that writing may include non-fiction, poetry, letters, and other types of writing. Students can use an asterisk to indicate writing that they have published in the classroom. Teachers can easily see how long a child worked on a particular piece by noting the date it was begun and the date it was finished. The form will then show both how much a child has written and how long he or she worked on each piece.

During individual conferences, students and teachers together can record the child's goal for writing on the third form. Progress toward those goals can then be assessed at the end of that term. These three forms can be stapled or glued to each child's Writing Folder.

The fourth Writing Folder form can be use by either a student or the teacher to document a student's growing grasp of writing skills and strategies. We'll briefly describe the four versions of the forms for recording students' writing skills.

The first form is blank so that you can record writing skills you notice during either formal or informal conferences. For instance, Carrie might record, "Uses capitals to start sentences" for one of her second graders. The advantage of the blank form is that it's flexible and won't be intimidating to students.

On the next version, Cindy Ruptic has included specific descriptors of skills she teaches in her multi-age primary classroom. She begins the year with only a few skills listed and add to the list as she teaches specific skills and her writers become more competent.

Patti Kamber's fifth graders fill out the next form themselves. Her version emphasizes higher level writing skills, such as using a variety of sentence structures and literary devices. Rather than dating the skill, Patti has provided a scale where students can record whether they can use the skill with guidance or independently. She finds that this form encourages students to assess their own skills and gives them a clear picture of how to improve their writing.

Patti designed the next form, called Writing Assessment, to parallel the Skills I Use form that her students complete. When she confers with her fifth graders, she notes their emerging skills and keeps the form in her Teacher's Notebook.

ASSESSING PROCESS WRITING

In *The Art of Teaching Writing* (1986), Lucy Calkins claims that "Teacher-student conferences are at the heart of teaching writing; it is through them that students learn to interact with their own writing." (p. 21) Teaching individual children in the context of their own writing can be effective and powerful. Learning to confer effectively with students takes practice and a great deal of intuition! You must have a good grasp of the stages of writing development and learn to teach responsively. The next series of forms may help you document specific skills and provide a structure for writing conferences.

TOPICS

PIECES I'VE WRITTEN

Begun	Title	Completed

* indicates a published piece

GOALS

Fall

Winter

Spring

SKILLS I USE

Skills	Date

Other comments:

SKILLS I USE

Skills	Dates:	With guidance«——»Independently
I label my pictures with words.		
I write phrases and sentences.		
I use my sounds to write.		
I use spaces between words.		
I use titles to tell my main idea.		
My writing has a clear beginning, middle and end.		
I use a variety of forms: journals;		
lists;		
observations;		
stories;		
poems;		
letters;		
reports;		
directions.		
I share my written work with others.		
I use spaces to show individual words.		
I write neatly.		
I use capital letters: to begin sentences;		
for proper names.		
I use punctuation: periods;		
question marks;		
exclamation points;		
quotation marks.		
I use the sounds of letters to help me spell.		
Other comments:		

SKILLS I USE

(Student Form)

Skills	Dates:	With guidance←——→Independently
Content:		
I select topics that interest me.		
I narrow my topics/have a controlling idea.		
I gather details/use a variety of sources.		
I select/develop appropriate significant relevant ideas.		
I put ideas in an order that makes sense.		
Style: I bring my writing to life with		
a natural, compelling, personal voice		
specific examples		
descriptive words		
strong, active words		
literary devices		
I present information clearly.		
I use a variety of sentence structures.		
My writing has momentum; it builds to a high point.		
My writing has an effective conclusion/resolution.		
Mechanics: My writing follows the conventions of		
spelling		
grammar		
punctuation		
capitalization		
paragraphing		
legibility		
Publication:		
I publish my writing.		
I share my writing with an audience.		
Other comments:		

WRITING ASSESSMENT
(Teacher Form)

Date_____ Name_____ Title of Piece_____

Skills Dates:	With guidance⟵——⟶Independently
Content:	
Selected topic that interested self.	
Narrowed topic/has a controlling idea.	
Gathered details/used a variety of sources.	
Selected/developed appropriate significant relevant ideas.	
Put ideas in an order that makes sense.	
Style: Brought writing to life with a natural, compelling, personal voice	
specific examples	
descriptive words	
strong, active words	
literary devices	
Presented information clearly.	
Used a variety of sentence structures.	
Built to a high point/has momentum.	
Has effective conclusion/resolution.	
Mechanics: Followed the conventions of spelling	
grammar	
punctuation	
capitalization	
paragraphing	
legibility	
Publication:	
Published piece.	
Shared with audience.	
Other comments:	

WRITING CONFERENCE RECORDS

Cindy Ruptic developed the first Writing Conference Record form on the next page to record children's progression in the early stages of writing development. (The stages match those on the Bainbridge Island Writing Continuum described in Chapter 13). Cindy circles, dates, or highlights the student's skill under the writing stages. For example, during a writing conference, she might record that Felicia is using mostly upper-case letters, and has just begun to use spacing between her words. In the columns below, she writes the date and anecdotal comments about the child's written piece or writing processes.

The grid at the left can be used to date wherever the child is in the writing process during that conference. For instance, Cindy notes that Ali just started a new piece of writing and Eric shared his ghost story at Author's Chair. She found that the checklist was much quicker than writing all the comments narratively. It's also very easy for her to transfer this information to the progress report each term. Cindy developed the first form to use with beginning writers. She included a sample so you could see how she fills out the form. She uses the second version with her more proficient writers.

WRITING CONVERSATIONS

Patti Kamber asks her fifth graders to complete the Writing Conversations form on page 88 before she calls students for a writing conference. She asks her students to think about which parts of their piece are working well and which parts are still a concern. They are asked to write what they have learned and what they will do next. These questions provide a structure for their conversations about writing.

Patti fills out the second Writing Conversations form during the actual writing conference. She uses the first column when students are in the planning stages for a new piece. She jots down notes in the second column when students share drafts with her. When students are ready to publish their writing, she transcribes their answers to the questions in the last column. Patti keeps these forms for each student in her Teacher's Notebook. These conversations provide Patti with information about individual students and ideas for mini-lessons.

ASSESSING SPELLING DEVELOPMENT

We assume you are familiar with the developmental stages of spelling. If not, we recommend three particularly excellent books on the topic: *Spel . . . is a Four-Letter Word* (Gentry, 1987), *Teaching Kids to Spell* (Gentry & Gillet, 1993), and *You Kan Red This! Spelling and Punctuation for Whole Language Classrooms, K-6* (Wilde, 1992). These books describe the stages of invented spelling in detail and provide excellent strategies for incorporating spelling into a whole language program. We'll briefly review the stages and describe the forms that we've used to assess spelling growth.

Developmental Stages of Spelling

Most children first experiment with writing by scribbling, or **pre-writing**. Children next experiment by using random strings of letters in the **pre-phonetic** stage. Writers at the **semi-phonetic** stage first use initial consonants, then start to use both beginning and ending consonants. Teachers usually breathe a sigh of relief when writers begin to rely on a **phonetic** approach. Teachers and parents can usually read a child's writing once they begin incorporating some middle consonants with a few vowels sprinkled in. **Transitional** spellers use the patterns of language, although not always correctly. The more students write and read, the more quickly they progress toward **conventional** spelling. The chart on the next page lists the

WRITING CONFERENCE RECORDS for _____ by _____ TERM _____

CONTINUUM

PRE-CONVENTIONAL	EMERGENT	DEVELOPING	BEGINNING
Scribble "writing"	Copies names/words	Directional conventions	Self=writer
Pictures	Pictures+print	Phrases	Complete thoughts
Labels w/"words"	Mainly upper case	Upper/lower case	Uses some punctuation
Random letter strings	Beginning/ending sounds	Spacing	Memoirs/Observations
	Tells about writing	Reads own writing	Others can read
		Invented spelling	Some conventional spelling

CONFERENCE NOTES   (Include under approximate level: Date, Title, Observations, Examples, Comments)

CHECKLIST

	Dates													
New Work														
Continued Work														
Pre-writing														
Drafting														
Proofreading														
Editing														
Revision														
Final Copy														
Published														
Authors'Chair														

WRITING CONFERENCE RECORDS for __Karen__ by __C. Hosey__ TERM __Spring__

CONTINUUM

PRE-CONVENTIONAL	EMERGENT	DEVELOPING	BEGINNING
Scribble "writing"	Copies names/words	• Directional conventions	• Self=writer
Pictures	Pictures+print	• Phrases	•• Complete thoughts
Labels w/"words"	Mainly upper case	• Upper/lower case	•• Uses some punctuation
Random letter strings	Beginning/ending sounds	•• Spacing	Memoirs/Observations
	Tells about writing	• Reads own writing	•• Others can read
		•• Invented spelling	• Some conventional spelling

CONFERENCE NOTES

(Include under approximate level: Date, Title, Observations, Examples, Comments)

Developing:

5/19 Book of SPY
CW
Pattern book
using some capitals
correctly

I spy a _____
conventional spellings
spy bed pizza
ring book flag
the end

Beginning:

5/25 Comic Book
New genre!
Detailed action
Pictures in collab-
oration w/Michael

Period—inconsistent
Exclamation point
Apostrophes in
contractions
* Dedication Page
& About the
Author assigned

CHECKLIST

	Dates		
New Work	5/10	5/25	
Continued Work	5/19		
Pre-writing			
Drafting			
Proofreading			
Editing			
Revision			
Final Copy	5/19		
Published	5/24		
Authors'Chair	5/24		

WRITING CONFERENCE RECORDS for_____ by_____ TERM _____

CONTINUUM

EXPANDING	BRIDGING	FLUENT	PROFICIENT	INDEPENDENT
Considers audience	Writes for varied purposes	Varies tone and mood	Adapts style for wider purposes	Writes cohesive pieces
Beginning/Middle/End	Adds literary devices	More complex sentence structure	Uses effective lit. devices	Internalizes writing process
Capitals/Periods	Uses spelling strategies	Connects paragraphs logically	Varies sentence complexity	Analyzes/evaluates writing
Add-on revision	Begins to sequence	Increased use of literary devices	Uses descriptive language	Perseveres through complex writing projects
Spells common words correctly	Begins to use paragraphs	Revises by adding examples	Revises for clarity	
Listens/gives others feedback	Proofreads/edits	Deletes when revising	Uses many revision strategies	
Edits punctuation, spelling		Edits with greater precision		

CONFERENCE NOTES

(Include under approximate level: Date, Title, Observations, Examples, Comments)

CHECKLIST

	Dates									
New Work										
Continued Work										
Pre-writing										
Drafting										
Proofreading										
Editing										
Revision										
Final Copy										
Published										
Authors'Chair										

Writing Conversations

Name _____

Title of Piece _____

Date(s)	Which parts do you feel good about?	What is a struggle or frustration?	What have you learned?	What will you do next?

Writing Conversations

FIRST CONFERENCE (IDEAS)	SECOND CONFERENCE (ROUGH DRAFT)	FINAL CONFERENCE (READY TO PUBLISH)
What are you going to write about?	How is it going?	How do you feel about this piece?
Who will your audience be?	What are you struggling with?	What is your favorite part?
What are your goals?	What have you learned?	What was the reaction of the audience?

stages of developmental spelling along with some specific examples. We've also listed the corresponding stages on the Bainbridge Island continuum.

One way to remember the progression is to observe how children who are just beginning to read first rely on their mouths to make the sounds of words. You can see this in many kindergarten and first grade classrooms as children voice the sounds they are writing. The progression is often from the mouth to the ear as children begin to write the sounds they hear. In the transitional stage, children rely on visual as well as auditory memory as they recall what a word "looks like" and "sounds like." One of the great joys of teaching young students is watching this remarkable progression unfold. Rather than correcting the spelling, we can celebrate a child's developing concepts about written language.

Developmental Stages of Spelling

Stage	Characteristic	Example	Continuum
Scribble Writing	letter-like marks	ᘢ ᣫ ᑯ ᘢ ᣫ ᣮ ～	
Pre-phonetic	random strings of letters	BMTYZ = WORD	Preconventional
Semi-phonetic	letter sounds, initial & end	WD or YD = WORD	Emergent
Phonetic	letter sounds, distinct words	WRD = WORD	Developing
Transitional	vowels, letter patterns	WERD = WORD	Beginning
Conventional		WORD	Expanding

The Conventions of Spelling Form

The Conventions of Spelling form can be used to assess spelling growth over time for beginning writers. Cindy Ruptic developed this form using ten words from Richard Gentry's article "*You* Can Analyze Developmental Spelling" in *Early Years K-8*, May, 1985. You may wish to develop your own lists of words that are challenging enough so that few of your students will spell them conventionally. The list must also include words that cannot be spelled phonetically in order to analyze a student's strategies. The words should not be ones that you have taught during the year in formal spelling programs.

Give the children the ten words as a "spelling test." We've provided you with a reproducible blank strip, numbered 1–10 where students can write the words. You can then staple the strips, one on top of the other, from fall, midyear, and in the spring. The advantage to using the strips is that you can clearly see changes without having to transcribe the students' spelling yourself. At the bottom of the form is a key you can use to code the types of miscues a student makes. Cindy Ruptic developed this key from Sandra Wilde's (1989) article in *The Whole Language Evaluation Book*. For instance, a child's errors might be primarily suffixes, such as using "t" instead of "ed" as shown in the example.

The Conventions of Spelling (10 Word Test) will help you clearly document each child's spelling growth. You may want to choose one child's spelling and make a chart such as the one on the previous page for Back to School Night. The chart shows the changes in one child's spelling from November to January to May.

	Fall	Winter	Spring
monster	mostr	moster	monster
united	younitid	united	unitide
dress	gras	drass	dress
bottom	botilm	botum	botume
hiked	hictc	hicet	hicte
human	wiemn	huomin	hwumin
eagle	egal	egol	egol
closed	closd	clousd	closde
bumped	bomte	bumt	bumped
type	tipe	tipe	tipe

Developmental Spelling Form

You can also use the Developmental Spelling form on page 95 with emergent writers. The developmental stages of spelling are listed across the top of the form with examples of how children at each stage would spell "word." (A variation of this form can also be found in the previous chapter on emerging readers and writers.) Specific examples of a child's spelling of words can be dated and copied under the appropriate column. You may prefer to photocopy and reduce student work, then glue the samples under the appropriate section. In either case, the result is a graphic representation of a student's spelling growth over time. This is another form that is useful for inservices or at Back to School Night.

Spelling Strategies Form

The Spelling Strategies form (page 96) was developed after reading the section on spelling in Linda Crafton's book, *Whole Language: Getting Started . . . Moving Forward* (Richard C. Owen, 1991). Many other books on process writing also describe a technique called "Guess and Go" or "Have a Go." Students are encouraged to write the word they are unsure about in several different ways. Students, as well as adults, often find that they can pick the correct spelling given several choices. This instructional tool encourages students to discuss spelling options. The form also provides diagnostic information, since the types of words students spell and the "guesses" they make reveal much about the students' strategies and understanding of written language.

Spelling Attitude Survey

Children's spelling ability and confidence are influenced by their perceptions of themselves as spellers and their understanding of what good spellers do. You can gain valuable information by interviewing intermediate students about spelling. Rather than include the form in this chapter, however, we have included it with the reading and writing interviews and surveys in Chapter 10.

Conventions of Spelling(10 Word Test) NAME_____

	WORDS	STUDENT WORK	Date:	Date:	Date:	Date:
1.	monster					
2.	united					
3.	dress					
4.	bottom					
5.	hiked					
6.	human					
7.	eagle					
8.	closed					
9.	bumped					
10.	type					

ERROR CODES: U=Unusual C=Consonants V=Vowels S=Suffix P=Permutation L=SingleLetter R=RealWord

Name_____

Date_____

1 --- monster

2 --- unintid

3 --- dress

4 --- bottome

5 --- hickt

6 --- human

7 --- egate

8 --- closed

9 --- bumt

10 --- tipe

NOTE TO TEACHER: After testing and collecting from students, cut out box with words and paste onto each child's **"10 Word Test"** form, gluing only along top edge.

Name_____

Date_____

1 -

2 -

3 -

4 -

5 -

6 -

7 -

8 -

9 -

10 -

DEVELOPMENTAL SPELLING

Name_____   Year_____

Date	PRE-PHONETC BMTYZ=WORD	SEMI-PHONETIC WD or YD=WORD	PHONETIC WRD=WORD	TRANSITIONAL WERD=WORD	CONVENTIONAL WORD=WORD	STRATEGIES EVIDENT

Strategy Codes:

A = Auditory
V = Visual
R = Rules
C = Conventional

SPELLING STRATEGIES

My Guess	Try Again	Ask Friends	Final Spelling

ASSESSING GROWTH IN REVISING AND EDITING

All too often writing instruction and testing has focused on editing skills. As any writer will confirm, revision is far more difficult than editing. As we tell students, the author is the only one who can revise; a secretary or word processor can help with editing. Revision is the process of trying to match what is in your heart and mind with what ends up on the paper. Revision focuses on meaning making. Whether we write a poem, a letter to the editor, a three-paragraph essay, or directions to a friend's house, our goal should be to communicate clearly. A process approach stresses that writing is most effective when it is done for authentic purposes and audiences. Children's author Mem Fox (1993) writes, "I wish I could discover what sorts of things my students care enough about to make them weep with worry as they try to get their writing right" (p. 8).

In a process approach or writing workshop, students may compose several drafts of a piece of writing. For emergent writers, revision may simply mean adding richer words or a bit more to a story. As writers become more accomplished, they may talk with adults or other students, read their writing aloud, and make notes on their drafts.

After students have revised their piece, they can switch gears and clean up the conventions. Editing consists of checking for correct usage of punctuation, grammar, and spelling. Your expectations will change depending on the age and proficiency of your students. As you teach new skills, you can raise the level of expectations. You can expect more from more proficient writers, particularly when they write for authentic purposes and audiences. Mem Fox (1993) adds, "The more I admire my potential readers, the more carefully I write and the more often I revise" (p. 9).

Revision and Editing Checklists

One hazard of creating checklists is that we can get locked into using one version instead of viewing forms as flexible. The next three editing forms are part of a series of six that Carrie Holloway and Cindy Ruptic use with their primary students at different times during the year. Their idea of flexible editing forms came from Jerry Miller, a teacher in Olympia, Washington. Carrie and Cindy begin the year by sharing their own published writing and describing how authors send for "Writer's Guidelines." The teachers explain how the editing forms are the Writer's Guidelines for their classroom.

In the fall, the form is very simple with only a few requirements. After discussing and modeling the new skills, Carrie and Cindy gradually increase their expectations of the young writers. Each successive form includes more complicated steps. The final editing form is used the spring and reflects the growing confidence and skills of the authors. We have included 3 editing forms in this book.*

Rather than giving all students the same form, you can give individual children different forms, depending on their level of proficiency. The idea of changing the content of a form as the year progresses is rather unique and helps bridge the gap between instruction and assessment. We want to stress, however, that the vocabulary and strategies on the form must be modeled and explained to students (sometimes over and over!) before you can expect them to use these forms successfully and independently.

The "Fix-It" Strategy

Children's growth in writing is very dramatic in elementary school. One simple technique that we've developed is the "Fix-It" strategy. Photocopy a writing sample from each of your

---

*Variations are on the disk under development for use with the book. Please see the end of the book for further details.

Dear Young Authors:

Before submitting your manuscript for publication, please check to see that you have conformed to our standards. Use this checklist.

WRITERS' GUIDELINES

☐ Title?

☐ Author's name?

☐ Copyright (digital) date?

☐ Page numbers?

☐ Clear spaces between words?

☐ I read my work with:
     1_____
     2_____

☐ This is my very best work
     (thinking, length, neatness)

When all boxes are checked, you may choose a cover to decorate your work.

When your work is complete, please submit it to our basket.

Thank you,
The Publishers

EDITING CHECKLIST

TITLE OF STORY_____ DATE_____

GENRE: Fiction Non-fiction Poetry Biography Autobiography

AUTHOR_____EDITOR_____

	Read to yourself
	Story makes sense
	Name on paper
	Date on paper
	Pages numbered
	Clear spaces between words
	Margins (2 cm surround)
	Periods
	Question marks
	Names capitalized
	This is my very best work: thinking, length, development, neatness
	Read to two others (signatures): 1)_____
	2)_____
	Other writing techniques to notice:

EDITING CHECKLIST

TITLE OF STORY_____ DATE_____

GENRE: Fiction   Non-fiction   Poetry   Biography   Autobiography

AUTHOR_____EDITOR_____

	Read to yourself
	Story makes sense
	Name on paper
	Date on paper
	Pages numbered
	Dedication page
	About the Author page
	Clear spaces between words
	Margins (2 cm surround)
	Periods
	Question marks
	Names capitalized
	Capitals at the beginning of sentences
	Paragraphs indented
	All sentences in paragraph about the same topic
	Spelling checker
	This is my very best work: thinking, length, development, neatness
	Read to two others (signatures): 1)_____
	2)_____
	Other writing techniques to notice:

students early in the fall. Be sure to date them and store them where you can find them easily! During individual writing conferences with students in the spring, show each child his/her writing sample from the fall with the instructions, "You wrote this quite a while ago. Show me what you've learned since then." Students can rewrite the piece, incorporating all the new strategies and skills they've learned over the year. This technique doesn't need a form or much preparation. You might want to then lay the two pieces of writing side by side and complete the "We Noticed" form described in Chapter 11.

On the next page we've included a student sample from a first grader. His first piece says, "I went to Disneyland and I got a teddy bear and I got a ice cream cone and it was cold." Notice Peter's discovery (and overuse!) of periods. He spelled some words phonetically, and he's just beginning to incorporate vowel sounds in his writing. Four months later Peter is using capital letters for "I" and using punctuation more appropriately. He's printing more neatly and leaving spaces between his words. Several times he replaced the "t" sound with "ed," perhaps overgeneralizing a new rule he learned about past tense word endings. Besides changing the spelling of many words ("dinelan" to "disnyland"), Peter displayed simple revision skills by adding "and I went by plane."

EVALUATING WRITING

In this chapter we've discussed ways in which to examine writing growth. One question that remains is how to determine how a child's writing fits into the big picture. A great deal of information about a child's specific strategies can be gathered using the assessment tools listed above. In addition, teachers may want to work with their students to develop specific criteria for evaluation. Large-scale writing evaluation most often uses holistic scoring or analytic scoring. Chapter 6 in *Windows Into Literacy* (Rhodes & Shanklin, 1993) provides a helpful description of these two techniques as they are used for large-scale analysis of writing. In your classroom, you may want to adapt these two techniques if you need to assign grades. We would hope that you would involve students in determining the criteria for grading and that students could choose the pieces to submit for evaluation.

Holistic assessment usually involves giving students a writing prompt and then giving papers one general score on a scale of 1–5 or 1–3. Analytic scoring rates particular aspects of a piece of writing, according to a predetermined set of standards. For instance, a report might receive four scores for the following categories: organization, content, mechanics, and creativity. Analytic scoring involves a scale, along with descriptors for each category. Both holistic and analytic scoring focus solely on evaluating written products. It's important to balance this perspective with information about a student's writing processes and attitudes.

In your class, you may want to have students develop the criteria for scoring particular types or aspects of writing. For example, if you are discussing leads, students could look at samples from literature and decide, on a scale of 1 to 3, how they would score each one. They can then evaluate the leads in their own writing. Interesting discussions can arise when students begin to look at the qualities of effective writing and apply that knowledge to their own work. We've found that intermediate students, particularly, like knowing the specifics of what makes good writing. The *Northwest Regional Educational Laboratory* in Portland, Oregon has developed some helpful tools for involving students in setting criteria and evaluating writing. Our concern is that if evaluation is stressed too heavily, writers may take fewer risks and begin to focus more on products than on the process of becoming better writers.

Whether you decide to use rating scales or not, the process of setting criteria with your students can help you analyze your values. This could apply to writing, reading, or other content areas. Patti Kamber, a fifth-grade teacher, writes:

PETER.   12-2

ł wt . to . Wihelan

and . i . gt .

aut a depar

and . i . gt .

tan li łembon .

and . it . wsolet .

PETER   4/22/93

T   I   WENED   tow   disny land   and
I   goed   a   tłty   bear   and
I   goed   a   Iserem con -
tow   and   I   WENEd   by   pllan .

Such discussions have helped me, as the teacher, to clarify instructional goals and expectations. Because students are part of the process, they feel more powerful and seem more motivated to make improvements in their work. At first, they seemed almost nervous about being allowed such responsibility. There were even a few children who thought I was not doing my job; that I should be the evaluator. A few teachers wondered if I was creating monsters, if children these days have too much power as it is. I believe that the criteria set to evaluate another person's work, however, should not be privy information. In fact, the criteria should be clear, written in large letters, and open to public scrutiny. Helping students set the criteria for evaluation can show students how to improve their work and grow as learners.

REFLECTION

Setting criteria leads nicely into the area of self-reflection. As the teacher, you may keep anecdotal notes during conferences, document spelling changes, and collect writing samples, but authentic evaluation should also include the child's perspective. It's important periodically to ask children what they are learning as writers. Children's comments provide insights that help us better understand their processes and provide appropriate instruction. For instance, Lisa Norwick asked her students, "What is the most recent thing you have learned to do as a writer?" One student wrote, "I learned to be even more descriptive by writing using similes and metaphors." When Lisa asked, "What do you want to learn next in order to be a better writer?" the student responded, "I want to learn to describe people's feelings and to use expressive language for dialogue, like bellowed and shrieked." Several assessment tools that encourage self-reflection, such as writing attitude surveys, are described in Chapter 10.

Writing Plans and After Writing

Our goal should be to nurture independent writers. One way in which we can encourage independence is to help students learn to use their writing time effectively. Patti Kamber uses the Writing Plans form on the next page to help students learn to monitor their efforts during writing workshop. Using this form, students set their goals for the writing time. At the end of writing workshop, the students complete the After Writing form, evaluating what went well, identifying problems, and coming up with a concrete goal for the next writing period. Patti uses the forms periodically throughout the year to monitor growing independence and sophistication in her students' responses.

Portfolio Writing Sample

The final form in this chapter is a reflection form that students can attach to the writing samples they select to include in their portfolios. Students can use a form like this one, or simply attach blank index cards or affix "Post-it" notes. If portfolios are truly student-owned, it's important for students to have a voice in each selection and to learn to articulate why they include each piece.

Students show tremendous growth in writing from kindergarten to the end of elementary school. We can document growth through observations and anecdotal notes, by recording skills and titles of writing pieces, by examining growth in the developmental stages of writing and spelling, and by encouraging self-reflection.

Writing Plans

Date_____ Name_____

My plans for writing today are_____

_____

_____

The area(s) in which I will be working is/are_____

_____

_____

The materials I need are_____

_____

_____

Writing Plans

Date_____ Name_____

My plans for writing today are_____

_____

_____

The area(s) in which I will be working is/are_____

_____

_____

The materials I need are_____

_____

_____

After Writing

Date_____ Name_____

I_____ in writing today.

Things that went well were _____

_____

_____

Difficulties I had were_____

_____

_____

Tomorrow I plan to_____

_____

- -

After Writing

Date_____ Name_____

I_____ in writing today.

Things that went well were _____

_____

_____

Difficulties I had were_____

_____

_____

Tomorrow I plan to_____

_____

PORTFOLIO WRITING SAMPLE   Date _____

Title:_____ by _____

Why did you choose this piece of writing to include in your portfolio?

_____

_____

How does this show your growth as a writer?

_____

_____

_____

What is your goal for writing?

_____

_____

PORTFOLIO WRITING SAMPLE   Date _____

Title:_____ by _____

Why did you choose this piece of writing to include in your portfolio?

_____

_____

How does this show your growth as a writer?

_____

_____

_____

What is your goal for writing?

_____

_____

CHAPTER EIGHT

Observing Reading Growth

One of the most fascinating aspects of teaching elementary school is watching children blossom as readers. This almost magical process, however, happens silently as a child turns the pages of a book. How much does that child know about print and reading? What connections is she making between the story and her own life? What strategies does she use when she encounters an unknown word? How is she growing as a reader? Traditional short-answer unit quizzes and standardized tests do not reveal the answers to these questions.

We have not included information on retelling and think-alouds. Hazel Brown and Brian Cambourne's book, *Read and Retell* (1987) provides a wealth of information on retelling as both an instructional and diagnostic tool. *Portfolios and Beyond* (Glazer & Brown, 1993) and *Windows Into Literacy* (Rhodes & Shanklin, 1993) provide detailed information on both retelling and think-alouds. Besides these techniques, you can also gather valuable information by observing students and talking to them about what they are learning. We've included information on anecdotal records in Chapter 5 and the forms for reading attitude surveys and self-evaluation in Chapter 10.

In this chapter, we will touch upon six methods of assessing reading growth and development: recording information from reading conferences, miscue analysis, running records, reading logs, response to literature, and self-reflection.

READING CONFERENCE RECORDS

We can learn a great deal by listening to children read aloud. Individual reading conferences are central to a literature-based reading program. During reading conferences, you can assess children's attitudes, strategies, fluency, and comprehension. It's important to remember, however, that as adults, we do most of our reading silently. We read more quickly and more efficiently when we read "to ourselves." For beginning readers in the primary grades, however, oral reading records can provide a helpful source of information about students' reading development.

Why Use Reading Conference Records?

The following series of Reading Conference Records can be used during individual weekly reading conferences. We developed the forms after finding we were recording the same anecdotal comments over and over. The forms enabled us to simply check off many areas, while still allowing room for comments. In addition, the checklist helps serve as a structure for watching and recording children's reading development. The Reading Conference Records provide valuable information about:

- which books students are reading
- levels of fluency
- students' attitudes toward reading
- strategies students use as they read aloud
- degree of comprehension

In addition, the structure of the forms allows you to

- comment positively on areas of growth
- teach specific skills/strategies individually
- help students with book selection
- encourage students to focus on meaning-making
- encourage self-evaluation
- jointly establish goals for reading
- provide a profile of reading ranges for the class

How Do You Use Reading Conference Records?

The first form (page 109) might be helpful if you are just trying oral reading records for the first time. Cindy Fulton developed this form to document each student's reading strategies, the degree of fluency and inflection, reading level, and level of comprehension. In addition, there is room for you to write comments and record any new strategies you introduce during the conference. We've included a sample of a completed Reading Conference Record from two conferences with a first grader on page 110.

Jan Peacoe, a special education teacher on Bainbridge Island, developed the second Reading Conference Record (page 111). In the first column, Jan writes the date of the conference and the title of the book. Next, she records any miscues the student makes, writing both the actual words from the text and what the student said. In the third column, Jan notes the skills or strategies she taught, then checks the level of fluency and comprehension. This simple form of miscue analysis could be used with readers of all ability levels. We've also provided a sample form Jan used with one of her students.

Initially, Cindy Ruptic's Reading Conference Record on page 113 looks intimidating, but it is actually easy to use. Cindy first records the date, title, and the child's name. On the left-hand side of the form are the stages of reading. Cindy has listed descriptors in simple terms across the row. (These stages and descriptors are the same ones used on the continuum described in Chapter 13.) As she listens to the child read, she circles or highlights the strategies the child is using. She records miscues under the appropriate column and jots down notes about strategies or concepts she introduces.

Cindy's first form could be used with beginning readers from the pre-conventional through expanding stages. She uses the second form (page 114) with her more fluent readers. The columns on this version focus less on decoding and more on comprehension strategies. Cindy has filled out a sample form on the bottom of each page.

When Do You Use Reading Conference Records?

You may want to use one of these forms whenever you hold a reading conference with a student. When you first begin reading conferences, you may want to try conferring with half of your class each week. Once you're comfortable with the process, weekly conferences work well. You may want to confer more often with children who are still struggling, new students, or students who have specific needs. Filling out one form a week will paint a fairly accurate portrait of a reader by the end of a grading period. If you keep the forms in your Teacher's Notebook, you can transfer the information to the progress report and share your conclusions with students and parents at conference time. It's helpful to support your observations with an audiotape or videotape of the student reading, as described in Chapter 3.

Reading Conference Record

Student_____

	Date:	Date:	Date:	Date:	Date:	Date:
	Title:	Title:	Title:	Title:	Title:	Title:
Level Appropriate						
Strategies: Whole idea						
Picture clues						
Pattern						
Sight Words						
First letter						
Decodes						
Context clues						
Skip/return						
Rereads						
Reads Fluently						
With Inflection						
Literal Comprehension						
Interpretive Comprehension						
Strategy Taught						
Comments						

CODES: + consistently
√ sometimes

Reading Conference Record

Student_____

	Date: 12/8	Date: 12/17	Date:	Date:	Date:	Date:
	Title: Two Little Dogs (G)	Title: Sleeping out (F)	Title:	Title:	Title:	Title:
Level Appropriate	Instructional Frustration ✓	Instructional Independent				
Strategies: Whole idea						
Picture clues	✓					
Pattern						
Sight Words	✓	✓				
First letter						
Decodes	✓	✓				
Context clues	✓	✓				
Skip/return						
Rereads	✓	✓				
Reads Fluently		✓				
With Inflection		✓				
Literal Comprehension	✓	+				
Interpretive Comprehension	✓	+				
Strategy Taught	contractions context	contractions speech marks				
Comments	door's = door is that's gate's won't = will not don't = do not isn't = is not I noticed you used context to self-correct over (after) the (they)	It's = it is what's = what is she's = she is Ways to show speech: Word bubbles speech marks (quotation marks)				

CODES: + consistenly
        √ sometimes

Name_____

READING CONFERENCE RECORD

Date and Title	Miscues & Comments book » said	Skills/Strategies Taught	Fluency	Comprehension	
				Factual	Inferred

Codes: + = Very Good
√ = Average
- = Needs Improvement

READING CONFERENCE RECORD

Name_____

Date and Title	Miscues & Comments book » said	Skills/Strategies Taught	Fluency	Comprehension	
				Factual	Inferred
10/19 The Witch's Christmas	with → witch, wreath → w, very → every	wr = r, Look at pictures	✓	+	✓
10/21 The Enormous Egg	me → my s/c, when → than ⟩ what makes sense?		–	✓	✓
10/26 scary stories	many miscues, Read to Damo Dani, Picked book from library·proud	Syllables, -oi	–	✓	✓
11/2 The Return of the 3rd Grade Ghostbusters	enough, check → jach, discovered how he could "read" periods → expression	gh = ph, context → expression	+	+	✓

Codes: + = Very Good
       ✓ = Average
       – = Needs Improvement

© 1993 Jan Peacoe, Bainbridge Island, WA

READING CONFERENCE RECORDS for_____by_____

Date:_____ Title(s):

EVALUATION OF READING	LEVEL:		Frustration	Instructional	Independent
PRE-CONVENTIONAL	Print concepts; Letter names; Focuses on pictures; Responds; Chooses/has favorites				
EMERGENT	Pictures to tell story; Names/words in context; Letter sounds; Memorizes pattern; Rhyme				
DEVELOPING	Self=reader; Word concept; Print+pictures; Simple words; Pattern books; Retells main idea				
BEGINNING	Level appro.; Sight words; Self-corrects; Punctuation; Phonics; Sentence structure; Context.				
EXPANDING	Many strategies; Short chapter books; Silently; Expression; Retells; Connects to experience				

Strategies, Questions & Evidence	Pictures	Pattern	Phonics	SightWords	Context	Miscues	SC	TG	I

*Strategy/Assignment: _____

CODES: SC=Self-Correct, TG=Teacher-Given, I=Ignored

Date: 12/8 Title(s): Two Little Dogs (Wright - G) 16 pages   Very difficult!

EVALUATION OF READING	LEVEL:		Frustration	← Instructional	Independent
PRE-CONVENTIONAL	Print concepts; Letter names; Focuses on pictures; Responds; Chooses/has favorites				
EMERGENT	Pictures to tell story; Names/words in context; Letter sounds; Memorizes pattern; Rhyme				
DEVELOPING	Self=reader; Word concept; Print+pictures; Simple words; Pattern books; Retells main idea				
BEGINNING	Level appro.; Sight words; Self-corrects; Punctuation; Phonics; Sentence structure; Context.				
EXPANDING	Many strategies; Short chapter books; Silently; Expression; Retells; Connects to experience				

Strategies, Questions & Evidence	Pictures	Pattern	Phonics	SightWords	Context	Miscues	SC	TG	I
Halting; working through text laboriously, but w/ good comprehension	gate's mouse rabbit		look door's that's good little bad him he way open	the we ran run	two	over (after) the (they) Beginning to use the context to self-correct	v v		
door's = door is thats's = that is gate's = gate is									
won't = will not don't = do not isn't = is not									

*Strategy/Assignment: 's and n't contractions / using context clues con: with
"I noticed" you're using text to help... text: text

© 1993 C. Ruptic, Bainbridge Island, WA   CODES: SC=Self-Correct, TG=Teacher-Given, I=Ignored

READING CONFERENCE RECORDS for_____by_____

Date: Title(s):

EVALUATION OF READING	LEVEL:	Frustration	Instructional	Independent
EXPANDING	Many strategies; Short chapter books; Silently; Expression; Retells; Connects to experience			
BRIDGING	Voluntary; Wider variety; Medium chapter books; silently; reads/understands most new words			
FLUENT	Young adult novels; Uses reference material; Literary elements/genre			
PROFICIENT	Rate; Complex YA novels; Literary discussions; Interpretive understanding; Library research			
INDEPENDENT	Evaluates, interprets, analyzes literary elements; Reads critically; Understands complex texts			

Strategies & Evidence	Connects to experience	Literary Elements/Genre	Vocabulary	Miscue	SC	TG	I

Response/Assignment: _____

CODES: SC=Self-Correct, TG=Teacher-Given, I=Ignored

Date: Title(s):

EVALUATION OF READING	LEVEL:	Frustration	Instructional	Independent
EXPANDING	Many strategies; Short chapter books; Silently; Expression; Retells; Connects to experience			
BRIDGING	Voluntary; Wider variety; Medium chapter books; silently; reads/understands most new words			
FLUENT	Young adult novels; Uses reference material; Literary elements/genre			
PROFICIENT	Rate; Complex YA novels; Literary discussions; Interpretive understanding; Library research			
INDEPENDENT	Evaluates, interprets, analyzes literary elements; Reads critically; Understands complex texts			

Strategies & Evidence	Connects to experience	Literary Elements/Genre	Vocabulary	Miscue	SC	TG	I

Response/Assignment: _____

CODES: SC=Self-Correct, TG=Teacher-Given, I=Ignored

ANALYZING MISCUES

A miscue is something said or read in place of the printed text. Ken Goodman (1969) first defined miscues as "windows on the reading process." He described children's deviations from the text when reading aloud as "miscues," rather than the more pejorative term, "mistakes." We don't expect readers to read with 100 percent accuracy, even as adults. It's not the number of miscues a reader makes that is important but the types of miscues. We're interested in whether the miscues affect meaning. A miscue analysis can reveal a student's concepts about reading and reading strategies.

What Is Miscue Analysis?

Miscue analysis is a practical, diagnostic assessment technique that complements the whole language curriculum. Miscue analysis helps reveal the strengths, weaknesses, and strategies a reader uses in processing written texts.

A variety of miscue inventories are available, from commercially published ones, to simplified teacher-made versions, to those more suitable for a researcher or clinician. Many are too complex and detailed for classroom use. *Windows Into Literacy* (Rhodes & Shanklin, 1993) and Dorothy Watson and Janice Henson's chapter in *Assessment and Evaluation in Whole Language Programs* (Harp, 1993), provide solid descriptions of this technique. We've developed an Informal Miscue Analysis (page 117) that is easy to use in the classroom with any type of text.

When Should You Use a Miscue Analysis?

Unless you are a Chapter I, Resource Room, or ESL teacher, you probably won't need to do a miscue analysis with every student. It requires making a copy of the text the child reads and can be rather time-consuming. A miscue analysis would be helpful, however, when a student is just learning to read or struggling with the reading process.

How Do You Analyze Miscues?

To analyze the miscues a student makes, you need to understand the cueing systems: graphophonic (letters/sounds), syntactic (grammar), semantic (meaning), and pragmatic (situational rules). You should also have a good understanding of reading strategies. We'd recommend taking a graduate reading class if these are not familiar terms. Several good books for strengthening your understanding in this area are Frank Smith's classic, *Understanding Reading: A Psycholinguistic Analysis of Reading and Learning to Read* (1988), Constance Weaver's book, *Reading Process and Practice: From Socio-Psycholinguistics to Whole Language* (1988), and *Readers and Writers with a Difference: A Holistic Approach to Teaching Learning Disabled and Remedial Students*, by Lynn Rhodes and Curt Dudley-Marling (1988).

Once you have a good understanding of reading, it's much easier to move from simply recording miscues and strategies to looking at patterns and making decisions for instruction. We've outlined a very simple procedure for analyzing miscues below, as well as a form for recording the information.

Directions for Informal Miscue Analysis

1. Let the student choose a passage from his/her textbook or literature book.
2. Photocopy the selection. (If a copy is not available, do a simple running record.)
3. Ask the student to read the passage aloud.
4. Record the student's miscues on the copy of the text. (It is helpful to also tape-record the reading.)

5. Ask the student to retell the passage. Score the retelling formally or informally to determine comprehension.
6. Afterwards, record the miscues on a summary sheet, then analyze the information to determine the student's reading abilities and needs.
7. Based on the results, develop instructional strategies to help the student become a more proficient reader.

Additional Comments

All too often, teachers and parents correct every word a child misreads or ask children to "sound it out" when they get to a word they don't know. Over-correcting can kill the pleasure of reading. Having to grunt and groan through unknown words can be drudgery for both readers and listeners. Relying on the graphophonics of a word by "sounding it out" is only useful for some words in English. Furthermore, it's only one of many strategies for figuring out unknown words. It's important to examine the types of miscues a child makes. Are they primarily nonsense words? Are the miscues graphically similar? Most important, do the miscues affect meaning? Accuracy is only part of the picture.

Pronouncing the word correctly does not guarantee that the word or passage is understood. Some readers may not make any miscues, but still not comprehend what they have read. Other children will make several miscues but still have a clear understanding of the text. These two patterns will have very different implications for instruction. You'll also want to document whether or not readers self-correct. If children do correct their own miscues, it shows they are focusing on making sense of what they read. The Informal Miscue Analysis form provides a helpful way of examining a child's miscue patterns and reading strategies.

RUNNING RECORDS

Although you may not regularly use miscue analysis with every student, you may want to do a running record. Developed by Marie Clay, this technique is simple and requires no preparation. Her two books, *The Early Detection of Reading Difficulties* (1988) and *An Observation Survey of Early Literacy Achievement* (1993), provide detailed descriptions of how to administer and score running records. Marie Clay (1993) states,

> You set yourself the task of recording everything that a child says and does as he tries to read the book you have chosen. Once you begin such recording, and after about two hours of initial practice, no matter how much you might be missing, you have made a good start. The more you take the records, the more you will notice about children's behavior. (p. 24)

During a reading conference, a student reads aloud from a book she has selected. Running records usually are based on a child's reading of 100 to 200 words. All you have to do is place a check by each word that is read correctly. When the student makes a miscue, simply record the word the student read. You may want to go back after the child has finished reading, and make a note of strategies and miscue patterns. We've provided a blank Running Record form and a completed example on pages 118 and 119.

INFORMAL MISCUE ANALYSIS

Name _____

Title _____

Page(s) _____

Teacher _____

Date _____

Words from Text	Miscues	Self corrects	Logically substitutes	Recognizes miscue	Graphically similar	Disrupts meaning	Non-word

RUNNING RECORD

Name _____

Title _____

Page(s) _____ Teacher _____ Date _____

On each line, make a check (√) for each word read correctly in that line or record miscues as read.

Line 1																													
Line																														
Line																														
Line																														
Line																														
Line																														
Line																														
Line																														
Line																														
Line																														
Line																														
Line																														
Line																														
Line																														
Line																														
Line																														
Line																														
Line																														
Line																														
Line																														
Line																														
Line																														
Line																														
Line																														
Line																														
Line																														
Line																														
Line																														
Line																														

RUNNING RECORD

Name __Terry Brady__

Title __Owl At Home "The Guest"__   Page(s) __6-7-8__   Date __2/14/92__

Teacher __C. Ruptic__

On each line, make a check (√) for each word read correctly in that line or record miscues as read.

Line 1	√	√	√	√	√				
Line 2	√	√	√	√					
Line 3	Who's —								
Line 4	√	√	√						
Line 5	√	√	√						
Line 6	√	√	√						
Line 7	√	√							
Line 8	√	√							
Line 9	√	√	√						
Line 10	√	√	√						
Line 11	√	√							
Line 12	√	√	√ afraid						
Line 13	√	√	√						
Line 14	√	√	√						
Line 15	√	√	√	√					
Line 16	√	√	√						
Line 17	√	√	√	√	√	√			
Line 18	√	√	√						
Line 19	√	√	√						
Line 20	√	√	√						
Line 21	√	√	√						
Line 22	√	√	√	√					
Line 23	√	√	√	√					
Line 24	√	√	√						
Line 25	√	√	√	√					
Line 26	√	√	√	√					
Line 27	√	√	√	√					
Line 28	√	√	√	√					
Line 29	√	√							
Line 30									

READING LOGS

A Reading Log is a useful tool for keeping track of the books a child reads. In the primary grades, a reading log might simply be a list of books that a child has read. At the intermediate level, reading logs can include the author, the date when the book was started and completed, and a rating of the book on a numerical scale. You may also want students to record the genre, the number of pages in the book, and possibly a brief reaction statement or comment. Children may want to record their favorite books.

Another way to use reading logs is to ask students to record the number of pages read every day for a period of time. They turn the log in when a book is completed. The child starts a new copy of the form with each new book.

Some of you may want to respond to students after they have read a number of books. You could write a brief note, suggest further reading, or recommend other titles or authors. The log then becomes a tool for a written conversation between you and your students. A dialogue journal, which we describe in the next section, is a more extensive form of written conversation.

Why Use Reading Logs?

Reading logs help paint a portrait of a child as a reader. Logs can be used to simply keep track of how much and what a student reads; however, this tool is more worthwhile if the logs become a way of examining the patterns of reading and sharing books with others. By recording the amounts and types of materials a student is reading, you can catch a glimpse of the child's interests, and the quantity and range of his/her reading. The information from reading logs can be useful in helping you and your students recognize reading patterns. By knowing what each student chooses to read, you can better match instruction to each child's level, rate, and interests. Information from the logs can also be shared with parents during conferences and in narrative comments on progress reports.

Logs become even more meaningful when you ask students periodically to look back at the list of titles they have recorded and choose favorites to share with other students. As adults, you probably have trouble remembering what you've read this year. We've found it helpful to keep our own reading log of chapter books (it's too hard to record all the picture books), adult novels, and professional books. You may even want to use one of the reading logs in this section for yourself!

When Are Reading Logs Used?

Reading logs may be used specifically for reading at home, reading in school, or a combination of both. You may wish to use the logs sporadically or only to record books on a topic or favorite books. *It's important to encourage extensive reading without allowing students to become competitive about the number of books they are reading!* The focus should never be on quantity over quality. Filling out the reading log is the student's responsibility and should never become a burdensome task that detracts from a child's pleasure in reading.

We have included five forms, ranging from the simplest to more detailed forms for older students or more proficient readers. We've also included a form where students can look back at their reading logs and record their favorite books. Finally, we included the Marine Science Reading Log to emphasize the notion that logs can tie into research and nonfiction reading. You can adapt the forms to fit your own themes and other content areas.

Do you keep the titles and authors of books you want to read or buy written on scraps of paper or worn-out "Post-it" notes? The last form in this series provides a place for you and your students to keep a running list of "books I want to read next." Students could keep this ongoing record in their reading folders. They can add to their list as students and teachers share favorite books and authors.

◣◣◣◣◣◣◣READING LOG◣◣◣◣◣◣◣

Name_____ Term_____

Date Completed	Title of Book	Author

READING LOG

Name _____

Month/Year _____

Title	Author	Start Date / Finish	Value High---Low	Genre	#of Pages	Response
			1 2 3 4 5			
			1 2 3 4 5			
			1 2 3 4 5			
			1 2 3 4 5			
			1 2 3 4 5			
			1 2 3 4 5			
			1 2 3 4 5			
			1 2 3 4 5			
			1 2 3 4 5			
			1 2 3 4 5			
			1 2 3 4 5			
			1 2 3 4 5			
			1 2 3 4 5			
			1 2 3 4 5			
			1 2 3 4 5			

DAILY READING LOG

Name _____

Date Started _____ Date Finished _____

Title _____

Author _____

Date	Pages Read	Event(s)	Response/Prediction

Here's why I love my favorites:

Title	Title
Author	Author
Reason	Reason

Title	Title
Author	Author
Reason	Reason

Title	Title
Author	Author
Reason	Reason

Here's why I love my favorites:

Hidi is My favrit book Becus iT has goTs and I Like goTs	The big book for Peace is one of My favrit book becos
	The name of The book is intasting
Marry crismas amilya badilya iS My favrit book Be cus IT has	A house foR a hermiT craB iS My farriT BooK Becus iT has a
SanTa clas inThe Book	hermit inThe Book

My Favorite Books

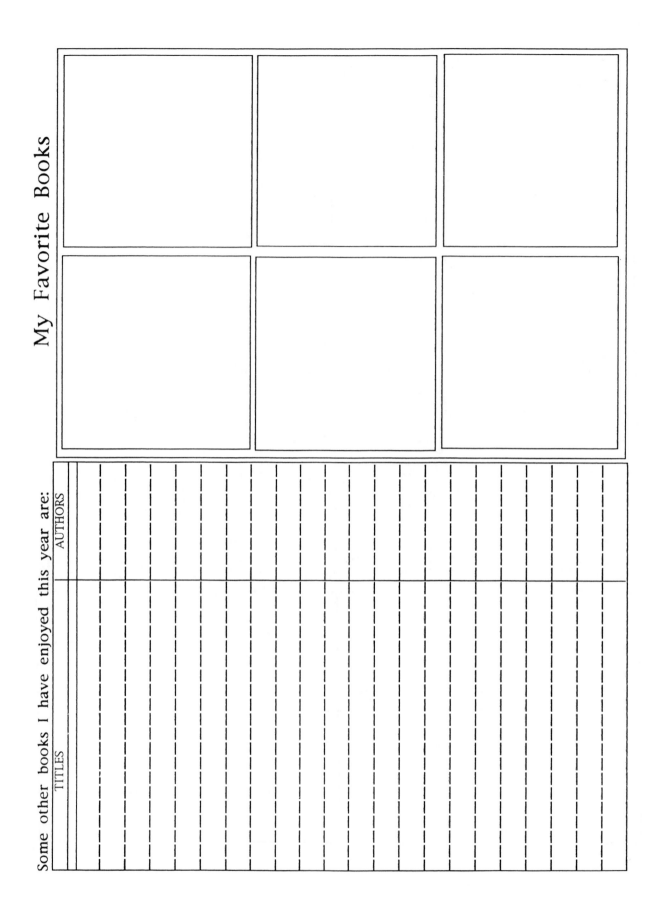

Some other books I have enjoyed this year are:

TITLES	AUTHORS

My Favorite Books

Some other books I have enjoyed this year are:

TITLES	AUTHORS		
hidin	Jax Spye		
The Big Book For Peace	Maurice		
Marry ChrismaS amilya	PeeGy PARISh		
A House for a Hermit Crab	ERiC CARNE		

🦀Marine Science Reading Log🦀

Name_____

Date	Title of Book	Author	Pages Read	Rating

🦀Marine Science Reading Log🦀

Name_____

Date	Title of Book	Author	Pages Read	Rating

Books to Read

Copyright	Title	Author	Genre	Description/Notes

RESPONSE TO LITERATURE

Many schools and districts are moving toward literature-based reading programs. Teachers have adapted the ideas of Lucy Calkins, Nancie Atwell, and Regie Routman and have developed Reader's Workshops. Teachers often begin the reading period with a mini-lesson, then model by reading their own book silently before moving around to confer with students. Students often share books at the end of the reading period. Most reading programs include time for quiet reading, time when students can read with each other, and time for the teacher to read aloud. Students also often have time to write about what they are reading in dialogue journals and create response projects about the books they complete.

You may wish to create Reading Folders like the Writing Folders described in the previous chapter. Reading Folders could include:

1. Goals (Chapter 7)
2. Reading Log (Chapter 8)
3. Strategies I Use (Chapter 8)
4. Interest Survey (Chapter 10)

The Goals form described in Chapter 7 on assessing writing could also be used during reading conferences. You may also want to select one of the Reading Log forms described above. We've next included a form for recording students' reading strategies on page 132, called Strategies I Use. The fourth form which you may decide to include in students' reading folder is an Interest Survey which you'll find in Chapter 10.

How Do Students Respond to Literature?

How were you most often asked to respond to reading in school? If you're over the age of 30, you probably only recall writing the answers to comprehension questions or filling in the blanks. If you are younger or were fortunate to have some imaginative teachers, you may have done an occasional play or diorama.

Over 35 years ago, Louise Rosenblatt first defined reading as a transaction that occurs as a reader interacts with the text. She also described two ways of reading: efferent and aesthetic. Short answer responses are usually efferent, focusing on what we learned from the story or passage. Aesthetic response, on the other hand, is what Rosenblatt (1978) calls the "lived-through" experience that incorporates a reader's emotions and personal reactions. In a literature-based program, students respond to many types of literature in varied ways.

Students may keep a dialogue journal in which they record written and artistic responses to what they are reading. They may choose final response projects using art, dance, writing, or drama. These artistic projects often require that students reread parts of the book and wrestle with meaning at a deeper level.

How do we know that students comprehend what they read? We now know that there are many ways to assess comprehension besides short-answer, literal level questioning. In this chapter we'll discuss how to encourage and assess response to literature.

What Are Literature Circles?

Literature circles are forums for discussing and reflecting on books students have read. Small groups of 4-6 students meet regularly to write and talk about books. These groups (sometimes called book clubs, story circles, or novel groups), will be referred to in this book as literature circles. All the students in the class may read one common book. At other times, small groups could read different books on a central theme or by one author. Sometimes, children in the same group may read different books on the same topic, such as the Civil War or endangered species. Literature circles may be led by either the teacher or the students.

Dialogue or response journals are often used in conjunction with literature circles. Students may write spontaneous reactions as they read or you may want to give the focus for their responses. These written responses can be the springboards for literature circle discussions. Literature circles take many forms, depending on the age of the students, your philosophy, and your knowledge of children's literature. For more information about literature circles, we suggest you read *Grand Conversations: Literature Groups in Action* (Peterson and Eeds, Scholastic, 1990).

Since more and more classrooms are moving toward a literature-based approach to teaching reading, we felt it was important to include a brief discussion of how literature circles work. We also wanted to provide a few forms that reflect how assessment can be incorporated into a literature-based approach.

Why Use Literature Circles?

The use of literature circles allows for greater exploration and reflection about a text than simply having students give short answers to predetermined questions with one "correct" response. Literature circles allow for individual interpretations and expose children to different perceptions of a text through conversation. In literature-based classrooms, students read a great deal and respond to literature through talking and writing. In addition, children may respond to literature aesthetically through art, drama, and music in journals and final response projects. A classroom that incorporates quality literature and response can encourage children to make connections and respond to what they are learning and reading in a variety of ways.

How Are Literature Circles Used?

Before you introduce literature circles to the class, it's important to develop an environment that encourages trust and risk-taking. It helps to spend time modeling procedures, how to keep a conversation going, and ways of listening and sharing in a supportive way. You may want to begin literature circles with a picture book or a book that you've read aloud. Initially you may feel more comfortable leading the literature circles and providing the focus for discussions and a structure for dialogue journals. With older students and with practice, you can remove the scaffolding and encourage students to take on more ownership of the literature circles.

At the beginning of the unit or week, you and your students "booktalk" the choices for literature circles. At first, there may only be two or three books, with several groups reading the same novel. Later in the year, you may have five or six choices. We have included an example of a form where students can record their first and second choices on a ballot. The Book Club Ballot on page 133 can reflect helpful information about the types and difficulty of books a student chooses. Once the groups are formed, you or your students decide how much to read each day and how often to meet.

The nature of literature circles depends on the reading level of students. Beginning readers may read one picture book a week, while more proficient readers may complete a chapter book over several weeks. Although students discuss elements of literature (character, plot, setting, etc.) at all levels, intermediate students are often able to talk about abstract concepts and themes convincingly. After completing a book, students may choose a response project to share with the class.

Literature Circle Self-Evaluation Forms

Carrie Holloway developed the forms on pages 134 to 136 for evaluating student participation in literature circles, which she calls book clubs. The Book Club Self-Evaluation form is a way of keeping her second graders focused and accountable during literature circles. Students record the date, and use the faces to record if they read the assignment, wrote in their journal, participated in the discussion, and listened to others.

The Story Activities Self-Evaluation form is another version that you can use with literature circles or other reading activities. Students complete the Story Activities Self-Evaluation form at the end of the week or when a project is completed.

Carrie has created a version of the same form that she fills out on each student. Called the Story Activities Evaluation, Carrie keeps this teacher version on a clipboard. At the end of the project, she files the forms in her Teacher's Notebook.

STRATEGIES I USE

Strategies	Date

Other comments:

☞☞☞Book Club Ballot☜☜☜

Write your first, second, and third book choice. Remember, if you do not get your first choice this time, you will next time. Be sure to sign your name!

First Choice _____

Second Choice _____

Third Choice _____

Name _____

- -

☞☞☞Book Club Ballot☜☜☜

Write your first, second, and third book choice. Remember, if you do not get your first choice this time, you will next time. Be sure to sign your name!

First Choice_____

Second Choice_____

Third Choice_____

Name_____

☜☜☜Book Club Self-Evaluation☜☜☜

Name_____Date Started_____Finished_____

Title of Book_____ Author_____

Directions: Evaluate yourself **each day** on how you did in book club.

☺ I did my best

😐 I did okay

☹ Not this time

Day	Date	Finished Reading Assignment	Wrote in Journal	Participated in Discussion	Listened to Others
1					
2					
3					
4					
5					
6					
7					
8					
9					
10					
11					
12					
13					
14					
15					

◐⬅ ⬛ ∅ Story Activities Evaluation ◐⬅ ⬛ ∅

(To be filled out by teacher)

Student Name_____ Date_____

Rating Scale: + Consistently/Independently
         √ With Guidance
         — Needs improvement

_____ 1. Student worked hard each day.

_____ 2. Student used time wisely each day.

_____ 3. Student cooperated and helped others.

_____ 4. Each project shows student's best effort.

_____ 5. Student chose projects that would challenge him/her.

◐⬅ ⬛ ∅ Story Activities Evaluation ◐⬅ ⬛ ∅

(To be filled out by teacher)

Student Name_____ Date_____

Rating Scale: + Consistently/Independently
         √ With guidance
         — Needs improvement

_____ 1. Student worked hard each day.

_____ 2. Student used time wisely each day.

_____ 3. Student cooperated and helped others.

_____ 4. Each project shows student's best effort.

_____ 5. Student chose projects that would challenge him/her.

Teacher's Record of Book Club

It's often helpful to have one page where you record information about the whole class. On the next form in this section, Carrie records information about each of her students. She writes the names of all her students in the first column. She then notes if each child completed the reading, contributed to discussions, listened to others in the group, and completed a journal entry. Carrie has room to add comments in the last column.

Literature Circle Evaluation Forms

Asking children to assess their preparation and participation in literature circles helps them become aware of patterns, learn the language for self-evaluation, and set goals.

On the Book Club Self-Evaluation form (page 138), students are asked to evaluate whether they were prepared and how well they participated in the group. The form also provides room for students to examine the strategies used when they read. Students can also note the focus of the discussion and their goals for the next literature circle meeting.

Mary Hadley's Novel Group Evaluation form on the followint page has room to record information about five students on one form. Her fifth graders can focus on fairly complex skills, such as accepting alternate points of view, using the text to support opinions, and making inferences. This form can be completed by a group facilitator or teacher.

The final Self-Evaluation for Literature Circles Form provides more open-ended questions than the previous forms. The version that you decide to use will depend on the ages of your students and their comfort with literature circles.

Literature Circle Response Log

Patti Kamber and her fifth-grade students developed the Literature Circle Response Log (page 141), which students complete as preparation for literature circles. Since her literature circles are student-led, the response log entries form the basis of their discussions. The form thus provides a scaffolding for students' written and oral responses to literature. You'll want to adapt the form to fit your grade level and the choices you have provided.

We've included two types of reproducible pages with space for illustrations and lines for written responses to literature.

Book Project Evaluation

Most students love doing final response projects, rather than formal book reports. Some examples of response projects are: talk show interviews with characters, readers' theatre, puppet plays, tableaus of scenes from a book, simulated interviews of authors, and alphabet books. The Book Project Evaluation form (page 144) could be filled out by the student or the teacher.

Literature Circle Debriefing Form

The last form in this set provides a way to help students learn to become better listeners and participate appropriately in a group. Discussions of what went well and how students could improve adds tremendous power to the potential of literature circles.

Teacher's Record of Book Club

Title _____

Date(s) _____

Name	Finished Reading	Discussion		Journal Entry	Other Observations
		Contributed	Listened		

✑📖✑📖 Book Club Self-Evaluation 📖✑📖✑

My name_____   Other group members:_____

Book title_____   _____

Author_____   _____

Date_____   _____

1. I completed my reading in the amount of time given.   **YES   NO**

2. If yes, list any strategies you used while reading. If no, write about what you think
    kept you from completing your reading in the agreed upon time.

    _____

    _____

    _____

    _____

3. I came prepared to discuss the book at the meeting(s).   **YES   NO**

4. My participation was:

Poor   **Okay**   **Great**
1   3   5

5. We talked about_____

    _____

    _____

    _____

    _____

6. My goal for my next book club is_____

    _____

☜☜☜Novel Group Evaluation☜☜☜

Novel_____ Author_____

Theme/Focus_____ Date_____

Names of participants	*				
Preparation					
Brought book and other necessary materials					
Read the assigned pages					
Noted excerpts to share (e.g. high interest, difficult, confusing)					
Participation					
Contributed to the dialogue					
Used higher-level, critical questioning					
Used text to support/clarify/question					
Elicited responses from others in group					
Presented/sought/accepted alternative points of view					
Inferred relationships not stated in text					
Referred meaningfully to story elements: plot					
characterization					
setting					
conflict					
theme					
mood					
symbol					
tension					

*Indicates person completing form

139

Self-Evaluation for Literature Circles

Name_____   Date_____

Use the following scale to rate yourself in each area: 1=Poor   3=Okay   5=Great

Reading the book	1	3	5
Literature Circle discussions	1	3	5
Dialogue Journal writing	1	3	5
Final Response Project	1	3	5

Which aspect did you enjoy most? Why?

_____

_____

_____

Where did you show the most improvement or what did you learn?

_____

_____

_____

What was difficult or challenging for you?

_____

_____

_____

What would you do differently next time?

_____

_____

What is your goal for the next literature circle set?

_____

_____

Other comments?

_____

_____

_____

Literature Circle Response Log

Name_____ Date_____

Title_____ Author_____ Pages_____

Summary

_____

_____

_____

_____

_____

My Reaction
What I thought about what I read...what I wondered...what was interesting...

_____

_____

_____

_____

_____

Points for Discussion
I'd like to talk to my group about...I'd like to ask them...I wonder...

_____

_____

_____

_____

_____

My goal for our next discussion is _____

_____

Name_____Date_____

Title_____

Author_____

Name_____Date_____

Title _____

Author_____

_____

_____

_____

_____

_____

_____

_____

_____

_____

_____

_____

_____

_____

_____

_____

_____

_____

■■■Book Project Evaluation■■■

Name_____ Date_____

Book Title_____

Author_____ Genre_____

Project Description_____

_____

_____

Check if: Comments:

☐ Materials used are appropriate to the project.   _____
                                                       _____
                                                       _____
☐ Project represents the book well.   _____
                                                       _____
                                                       _____
☐ Project shows care in production.   _____

■■■Book Project Evaluation■■■

Name_____ Date_____

Book Title_____

Author_____ Genre_____

Project Description_____

_____

_____

Check if: Comments:

☐ Materials used are appropriate to the project.   _____
                                                       _____
                                                       _____
☐ Project represents the book well.   _____
                                                       _____
                                                       _____
☐ Project shows care in production.   _____

Literature Circle Debriefing

Name_____ Date_____

Title_____ Author_____

My Group:

Today's discussion was_____

because_____

_____

_____

We could improve by_____

_____

_____

Me:

My attitude in literature circles today was_____

because_____

_____

My participation was _____

because_____

_____

I could improve by/if_____

_____

_____

_____

REFLECTION

Besides noting students' reading strategies and listening to them read and respond to books, you also need to ask children what they are learning as readers. In Chapter 10 we focus on many different ways to involve students in self-reflection and self-evaluation. Here we've included our last two forms that specifically relate to reading.

Portfolio Reading Tapes

Students can fill out the next form to accompany an audiotape of their oral reading. They record why they chose the book to read and how the tape shows their growth as readers. Next, they write their goal for reading. We've found that children become better able to monitor their fluency and expression when they hear a tape of themselves reading aloud.

Portfolio Reading Response

Students can use the final reflection form to attach to reading responses they include in their portfolios. Reading responses could be written pieces from their dialogue journals, artistic responses, scripts from plays, or puppets from a literature response project. Students may want to include photographs of projects that do not fit in the portfolio. You may want to encourage students to include both efferent and aesthetic responses.

In this chapter we've presented a variety of forms for assessing reading growth through reading aloud, reading logs, literature circles, dialogue journals, response projects, and portfolio entries. You'll need to decide which of these forms best suits your program and the ages of your students. Remember not to overdo the forms; be selective.

_____ TAPED READING of _____ by _____
(Date)   (Title)   (Name)

Why did you choose this book to read and have taped?

_____

_____

_____

How does this show your growth as a reader?

_____

_____

_____

What is your goal for reading?

_____

_____

_____ TAPED READING of _____ by _____
(Date)   (Title)   (Name)

Why did you choose this book to read and have taped?

_____

_____

_____

How does this show your growth as a reader?

_____

_____

_____

What is your goal for reading?

_____

_____

_____'S PORTFOLIO READING RESPONSE   Date_____

(Name)

Title:_____Author:_____

Why did you choose this reading response to include in your portfolio?

_____

_____

_____

What does this show about your growth as a reader/writer?

_____

_____

_____

_____

_____'S PORTFOLIO READING RESPONSE   Date_____

(Name)

Title:_____Author:_____

Why did you choose this reading response to include in your portfolio?

_____

_____

_____

What does this show about your growth as a reader/writer?

_____

_____

_____

_____

CHAPTER NINE

Assessment in Content Areas

Most of the books on authentic assessment focus solely on literacy. At the elementary level, this is not surprising, since for many teachers, reading and writing are our strong suits. Although writing across the curriculum has gained acceptance, assessment across the curriculum is virtually unexplored. Most books on assessment mention portfolios as containers for work from all areas of the curriculum, but teachers are left without specific help. A fifth grader spurred our thinking when he commented in his self-reflection, "I want to be a scientist and my portfolio doesn't show that!" It's important that we begin to explore how to include content area learning in student portfolios.

On Bainbridge Island, teachers have been focusing on exploring issues of literacy assessment. Ideas about assessment in content areas are just beginning. We need much more information in this area. One of the challenges of content area assessment is that the types of processes and products vary greatly. We hope you can use our ideas as a framework for creating forms to fit your own unique assignments and projects. We encourage you to send us the forms you have developed as we continue to explore strategies for assessing learning in content areas.

What do you think of when you picture social studies in fifth or sixth grade? Most of you will probably recall research reports on Mexico or Argentina. You probably copied facts from encyclopedias, and spent a great deal of time the night before the report was due on colored pencil maps and a neatly lettered cover. The focus was on finding and copying facts, rather than on understanding the culture and history of another era or country.

Many teachers approach history and geography differently today. Students can interview guest speakers, use databases to access current information, and read current newspaper articles and historical fiction. Instead of standard research reports, students may choose to share what they have learned through travel brochures, murals, video talk shows, or alphabet books. How can such a wide range of projects be evaluated? The National Council for the Teaching of Mathematics and the National Science Foundation are two groups that are currently exploring alternative assessment in the content areas. New books are just appearing which apply a writing workshop/process approach to science (Saul, et al., 1993), math (Bickmore-Brand, 1990), and history (Jorgensen, 1993; Tunnell & Ammon, 1993). These approaches focus on the process of inquiry, critical thinking, and problem-solving using authentic texts and meaningful activities. Brief mention is made in these books about the role of assessment, but much more is needed.

CONTENT AREA LEARNING

To discover how much students have learned, you can evaluate either the process or the product. One powerful way to evaluate process learning is through self-evaluation forms. In the next chapter, we have included self-evaluation forms for math and science. The information from these surveys may provide helpful information about your student's attitudes and experience in those content areas. You may also want to have students keep Process Journals or learning logs in which they reflect on their questions and insights in content areas.

It's important that you are clear about the goals of your content area curriculum and how students can demonstrate they understand the material and concepts. It may be perfectly reasonable to measure some types of learning through multiple choice or short answer tests. Critical thinking, understanding of broad concepts, problem solving and performance skills, however, need to be assessed in a variety of ways. Assessment will be most representative of student learning when the tasks are a part of ongoing instruction and involve authentic tasks and purposes.

When students work collaboratively, it's challenging to measure what each individual has learned. How can you know who contributed what? In addition, how can you measure what each participant retained? Observe students as they work together. Keep anecdotal notes and talk with students. You may also want to have peer evaluations when students are working in group situations, although great care must be taken to maintain a positive focus and supportive environment.

You probably complete units or themes with some type of final project. Besides observing students and asking them to evaluate their process, you can also involve students in setting up the criteria for evaluation. When the assignment is first given, ask your students: What do you think would make a project outstanding or worth an "A"? The process of articulating the criteria will not only give them clear expectations, but will also give them a sense of ownership. They can then evaluate themselves, using the specified criteria they developed. At the same time, you can evaluate the students by their own criteria. During individual conferences you can compare your evaluations and discuss discrepancies. As we said in Chapter 8, students continually surprise us with their honesty. They are usually harder on themselves than we would be.

The results from student evaluations will also provide you with valuable information about the assignment and your curriculum. Your discoveries will likely affect what you teach next and perhaps how you will approach the same assignment next year. Assessment and instruction are inextricably interwoven.

How Are Content Area Assessment Forms Used?

You will need to adapt the forms we've provided to meet the needs and ages of your students, skills and strategies that you teach, and your specific assignments. The forms could be modified slightly to be filled out by the student, by peers, or by the teacher. It's important to remember, however, that the product is only part of the picture. We urge you to also include a self-reflection component in which students can discuss obstacles, insights, and understanding gleaned during the learning process.

PROJECT AND PROBLEM SOLVING EVALUATION FORMS

Pictures liven up a portfolio. You can glue photographs of final projects or students at work on the first form, called Here I Am. Primary students can dictate or write about what they are doing in the picture and why it's important. Older students may want to include a picture with more room for comments.

The next three forms could be helpful in assessing intermediate grade students' problem-solving strategies. The focus is not on assessing whether students achieved the "correct answer," but to gain information about the problem-solving processes students employed. You could adapt the scale and categories to suit the particular assignment. The Problem-Solving Evaluation form could be easily used in math, science, or cooperative learning activities.

The student, teacher, or peers could use the Project Evaluation form (page 155) to evaluate any type of project that involved a written paper and an oral presentation. If the teacher and student both evaluated the project, they could compare and discuss scores before arriving at a final grade. Each of these forms encourages students to evaluate their own processes and products.

The Project Check-Up form (page 156) could be used with a variety of projects or assignments. The questions prompt students to think metacognitively about what they have learned. If used before the project is completed, the form also provides a place for students to specifically ask the teacher for help. This final form, in particular, focuses students on the process of learning and encourages self-reflection.

We designed these forms to evaluate a variety of projects. The final set of forms, in contrast, are very specific in nature. Very few of you will be doing architecture or marine science projects at these specific grade levels! They are only included as examples.

As teachers move toward an integrated curriculum, the lines between reading, writing, and content area learning begin to blur. We hope that these very specific forms encourage you to develop evaluation tools for the themes and projects in your own classroom. Please send us copies of your content area forms!

ARCHITECTURE EVALUATION FORMS

Patti Kamber developed the forms on pages 158–160 as part of her architecture unit in fifth grade. After speaking to architects, studying architecture, perspective drawing and scale, students designed and built a three-dimensional structure. The project involved learning in measurement, geometry, social studies, and history. The Architecture Evaluation form was a final reflection about both the product and process. We've included a completed form on page 159. Note such comments as, "I thought architecture was excellent because I'm not a worksheet kind of a person."!

Before students had completed their building, they spent quite a bit of time in small groups developing and discussing the criteria for evaluation. Both Patti and her students filled out the Architecture Project Rating independently. Patti then conferred with each student; they compared their scores and discussed any discrepancies. Together they negotiated the final grade for the project. The towering structures the students created were incredible and showed the hours of time each of them spent on the project. Students felt a great sense of pride because they had been involved in determining the standards, had a voice in their own evaluation, and had a great deal of freedom in the assignment.

MARINE SCIENCE EVALUATION FORMS

Carrie Holloway spends several weeks each year on a Marine Science unit with her second graders. Her Marine Science Book Plan (page 161) is a contract where students decide which sea animal they will research and the books they will use.

Besides their primary research book on the sea animal they have chosen, Carrie also requires students to read several other books about marine science. She collects many library books, both fiction and nonfiction, with a wide range of reading levels. By the time Carrie begins this unit in the spring, her students are quite comfortable with the procedures for literature circles. Her students record the title, author, number of pages read, and rate the book on the Marine Science Reading Log (Chapter 8). The difficulty of the books students choose and the amount they read provide Carrie with helpful information. She further checks comprehension during individual reading conferences.

PRIMARY MATH EVALUATION

A group of first-grade teachers on Bainbridge Island developed the last evaluation tool in this chapter to assess their primary students' understanding of math skills and concepts. The items on this screening tool are ones that match most primary math curriculums. Teachers use a different color pen each time they evaluate students and write the date in the box at the top of the page. They simply circle or check what the child can do. The next time the teacher evaluates that child, he or she uses another color pen in order to graphically show growth on one page. The form could be completed by the teacher each term. You could adapt the same form for use with intermediate students. This form, however, only evaluates skills.

In her article called "The Intellectual Costs of Secrecy in Mathematics Assessment," Judah Schwartz (1991) describes the limitations of traditional math tests. Schwartz suggests that multiple-choice tests ask students to recognize rather than produce answers and states,

> If we use tests that ask students to recognize answers rather than construct solutions, we will be teaching students tricks for recognizing answers rather than strategies for constructing solutions . . . If we use tests that suppress subtlety and nuance, we should not be surprised that our students' analyses tend to be superficial and simplistic. (p. 137)

It's important to examine process as well as products and "right answers." Just as you can learn a great deal by watching children engaged in actual reading and writing tasks, it's important to take the time to listen to children as they investigate the world of mathematics. You may want to begin by taking anecdotal notes as children experiment with manipulatives and work together to solve problems. As you become more aware of the patterns of development in numeracy, you can begin to identify benchmarks and characteristics of growth at various stages. You may also want to introduce math journals or logs where students can evaluate their own growth and identify areas of confusion.

The teachers on Bainbridge Island are working this year on math and science continuums, much like the reading and writing continuums described in Chapter 13. They hope the focus on the developmental nature of inquiry and numeracy with specific descriptors will better reflect students' growth in mathematics and science. It's hard to move past the traditional emphasis on skills. It's important that a continuum not become a linear list of skills, but also include problem solving, strategies, an emphasis on process, and a variety of types of inquiry. The forms provided here are merely a beginning. We hope you send us any continuums and forms your school or district has developed.

We hope that the architecture, marine science, and math assessment forms provide ideas about how you could design similar tools for assessment in other content areas.

Here I am...

I am _____

This is important because _____

...in _____

Signed _____

Date _____

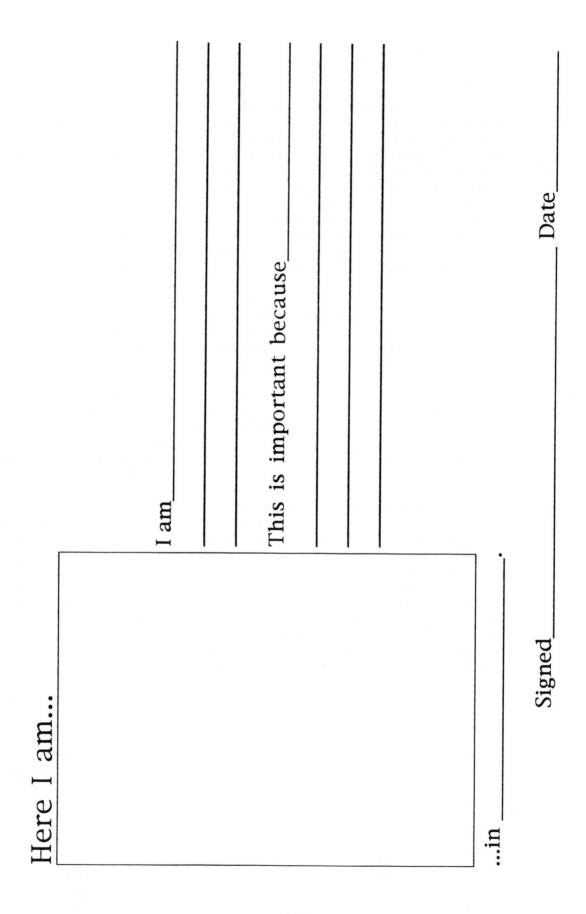

Problem Solving Evaluation

Name_____ Date _____

Activity_____

1. Tell briefly how you approached the problem. What were the strategies and/or techniques that you used to get started?

   _____

   _____

   _____

   _____

2. What different ways did you organize all of your materials/information?

   _____

   _____

   _____

   _____

3. How did you solve the problem? What techniques made you feel successful?

   _____

   _____

   _____

   _____

4. How do you feel about the way the process worked for you? What are some things that might have made it easier for you? What were some strategies other students used that made sense to you?

   _____

   _____

   _____

   _____

Project Evaluation

Name_____ Date_____

Project Description _____

1 = Poor

2 = Fair

3 = Okay

4 = Good

5 = Great

1 2 3 4 5   **Quality of Ideas** (includes important concepts in writing and illustrations, maps, graphs and/or models)

1 2 3 4 5   **Expression of Ideas** (introduces topic, develops topic, has an appropriate conclusion)

1 2 3 4 5   **Creativity** (expands assignment, is visually interesting, shows creativity)

1 2 3 4 5   **Conventions** (uses conventional spelling, punctuation and grammar, shows effort in editing, polished final product)

1 2 3 4 5   **Clear Presentation** (organized, audible, clearly explained)

1 2 3 4 5   **Participation** (communicated clearly, shared in the work, listened to others)

Comments: _____

_____

_____

_____

_____

_____

_____

Project Check-Up

Name_____ Date_____

1. My project/assignment is _____

_____

_____

2. I accomplished _____

_____

_____

3. I learned (list at least two things) _____

_____

_____

_____

_____

_____

_____

4. I feel good about _____

_____

_____

_____

5. I need help with _____

_____

_____

_____

6. My next goal is _____

_____

_____

Architecture Evaluation

Name_____   Date_____

My project was _____

_____

I built this because _____

_____

_____

_____

While I was building, the best part was _____

_____

_____

_____

The parts that were difficult were _____

_____

_____

_____

The thing I like best about the finished project is ____

_____

_____

I think architecture is_____, because

_____

_____

I learned _____

_____

_____

▦▦▦Architecture Evaluation▦▦▦

Name_____ Date _2-23-93_

My project was ___a futuristic monorail_____

I built this because ___we have to do something about_
_rush hour_____

While I was building, the best part was __building it___
_and finding out my ideas were good_____

The parts that were difficult were ____figuring out the_
_scale!_____

The thing I like best about the finished project is ___people_
_saying wow! who built that?_____

I think architecture is____excellent_____, because
___I'm not a worksheet kind of a person_____

I learned ___that the older you get the easier life is because
_you do things you really need to do_____

▐█▟▄▛ Architecture Project Ratings ▟▛▄█▌

Name _____ Date _____

Criteria	Point Range	Student	Teacher	Final
Durability	1-3			
Aesthetics	1-3			
Matches Floor Plan	1-3			
Accurate/Precise building	1-3			
On time	0-1			
Time spent on project outside of class	0-3			
Extras	0-3			
Organized folder	0-1			
Total possible	20			

Additional comments:_____

_____

_____

_____

_____

_____

_____

❧Marine Science Book Plan❧

Name_____ Date _____

The sea animal I'd like to learn about is _____

One book I'm going to read is called _____

It is written by_____ and has _____pages.

(number of last page)

☞ You will only have 4 or 5 days to read.

1. I think I can read (check one):

 All of it

OR

 Only these parts (list chapters and/or page numbers):

_____

_____

_____

2. I will read at least _____ pages each day.

(how many?)

3. I plan to work _____.

(alone or with whom?)

4. I might need help with _____

_____

_____

Remember: When you read you should find 2 or 3 interesting places to mark with "Post-it" notes so you can share with your literature circle.

PRIMARY MATH Individual Student Composite Record for_____Homeroom_____

Date (color code):					

NUMERALS/PLACE VALUE

Numeral Recognition	(circle) 0 1 2 3 4 5 6 7 8 9 10 11 12 Teens 20-99 100 1000	
Numeral Form	(circle) 0 1 2 3 4 5 6 7 8 9	
Reading Numbers	(circle) 13 31 40 87 15 21 137 350 249 306 113 415 710 609 530 999 1000	
Writing Numbers	(circle) 14 41 50 97 16 31 147 349 100 204 314 140 210 111 1000	
Reads a model for	(check)	10's and 1's	100's, 10's and 1's
Writes a model for	(check)	10's and 1's	100's, 10's and 1's

COUNTING

One-to-one correspondence	(check "to...")				
Counts by 1's	(check)	to 10	to 20	to 100	past 100
Counts by 5's	(check)		to ___	to 100	past 100
Counts by 10's	(check)		to ___	to 100	past 100
Counts by 2's	(check)		to ___	to 100	past 100
Counts backward	(check)	from 10	from 20		
Counting on	(check)	from 5	from 10	from 25	from 100

ARITHMETIC

Concept ("hiding")	(circle)	3 4 5 6 7 8 9 10
Additon facts to 10	(circle)	3 4 5 6 7 8 9 10
Addition facts to 18	(circle)	11 12 13 14 15 16 17 18
Subtraction facts to 10	(circle)	3 4 5 6 7 8 9 10
Subtraction facts to 18	(circle)	11 12 13 14 15 16 17 18
Two-digit addition w/regrouping	(circle)	w/guidance developing consistently
Two-digit subtraction w/regrouping	(circle)	w/guidance developing consistently

MEASURING

Linear/non-conventional	(date observed/example)					
Linear/conventional	(check)		metric		customary	
Fractional	(check)	halves	quarters	eighths	thirds	tenths
Time	(check)	hour	half-hour	quarter past	quarter 'til	to minute
Money	(check)	penny	nickel	dime	quarter	
	Sets of:	1¢	5¢	10¢	25¢	
		1¢ and 5¢	1¢ and 10¢	5¢ and 10¢	1¢, 5¢ and 10¢	

GEOMETRY

Explorations	(date observed/example)

PATTERNS/FUNCTION

Concepts	(check)	recognizes	reproduces	extends	creates
Explorations	(date observed/example)				

GRAPHING/COMPARING

Sorting	(check)	sorts	names rule	re-sorts
Comparing	(check)	equals	more	less
Graphing	(check)	interprets	records	creates
Explorations	(date observed/example)			

LOGIC/PROBLEM SOLVING

Uses math to solve real problems	(date observed/example)
Explorations	(date observed/example)

CHAPTER TEN

Involving Students in Assessment

We feel very strongly that students should be actively involved in assessing and evaluating their own growth and learning. This chapter is divided into five sections. In the first part we'll address the role of self-assessment and provide an example of how metacognitive thinking can develop over time. We will then discuss four other areas: self-portraits, attitude surveys, interest surveys, and self-reflections. You may want to start involving students by using an interest or attitude survey. As your assessment program develops, you can move toward involving students in more decision-making and self-reflection.

Defining Terminology

As we've read recent articles and books on assessment and evaluation, we've been confused by the terms that authors seem to use interchangeably. In Chapter 2, we defined the differences between assessment, evaluation, and reporting. In this chapter it seems appropriate to distinguish between self-assessment, self-evaluation, and self-reflection. Although the differences may seem minute, the process of examining each word helped clarify our thoughts. We have developed a graphic representation of the relationship of these three terms (see Figure 10-1).

Self-reflection is at the top of the figure, since it seems the broadest in nature. Reflection is a thoughtful contemplation of learning. Questions of self-reflection are more aesthetic and focus on emotions and feelings, as well as thoughts. A learner might ask, "What did I learn?", "How do I feel about my learning?" and "What new discoveries have I made about myself and the world around me?"

The process of self-assessment seems to focus on both the process and products of learning. Self-assessment might involve questions such as, "How do I learn best?" and "How am I growing?" Forms and questions that involve self-assessment seem to focus more on the ongoing process of learning.

Each term or at the end of a project, it seems more appropriate to focus on questions of evaluation. Learners might ask themselves, "How did I do?", "How have I improved in this area?", "What are my areas of strength and areas for growth?", and "Where do I stand in the large picture?" Self-evaluation questions seem more summative in nature and involve more appraisal.

Self-reflection, self-assessment, and self-evaluation are three of the cornerstones of metacognition and should lead learners to a greater awareness and understanding of themselves. In addition, the processes should provide insights that enable students to set their own goals. Students can learn to articulate what they hope to learn next and their plan of action.

We've tried to show these distinctions graphically, although we realize that all four processes are interwoven.

PROBLEMS WITH SELF-EVALUATION

In graduate classes when teachers are asked what grade they feel they've earned, they usually feel very uncomfortable. We're not used to being asked to evaluate ourselves. Self-evaluation is a skill that requires modeling, discussion, and practice.

The first barrier to self-evaluation is that students may simply give us the answer they think we want to hear. The only way to counteract this tendency is to assure students that we really want their honest opinion. You'll need to model self-reflection with think-alouds and mini-lessons. You may want to use examples from your own reading and writing, and think-aloud your strategies and processes. You can also use student examples of self-reflection and self-evaluation from previous years (with the author's permission). It's important to keep in mind that students will only be willing to respond honestly if the environment you've created encourages risk-taking. Students need to recognize that you genuinely want to know about how they learn in order to support them.

The second hazard is that most young children simply don't have the metacognitive vocabulary to articulate how they learn. You'll need to introduce some terminology and do a great deal of demonstration. Although intermediate students may have the language for self-reflection, reading and writing may have become so automatic that it's hard for them to step back and reflect upon their processes. They may also be less familiar with "school language" and questioning.

I firmly believe that children are experts on their own learning. However, it is my experience that some children do not as readily articulate responses to explicit ques-

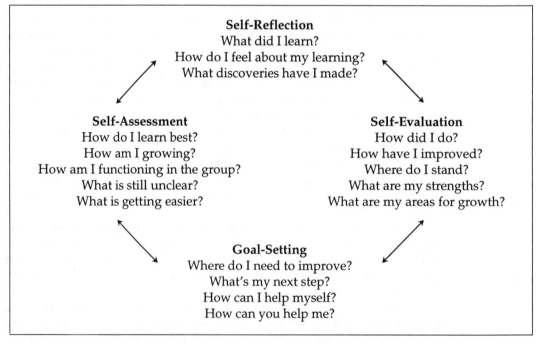

Figure 10-1   Self-reflection, self-assessment, self-evaluation, and goal-setting.

tioning of their writing process or thought patterns. Human beings, adults and children alike, can generally do a thing before they can talk about the doing. With young children, the bounds of their emergent language make it even harder for them to articulate what they can do. Children from non-mainstream homes, who are not socialized into the school-based literacy patterns of book talk (which precede portfolio talk) also have difficulty responding to explicit questions about their learning.

(Matthews, 1992, p. 169)

One surprising aspect of involving students in assessing and evaluating themselves is the honesty they display and the insights that you can gain from their reflections. Self-reflection is a powerful technique, but it must be modeled and taught.

BENEFITS OF SELF-EVALUATION

Opportunities for self-reflection and evaluation are essential to encourage responsibility for learning, to promote critical thinking, and to help students become actively involved in their own education. By giving children frequent opportunities to reflect upon and evaluate their progress, they can develop skills that allow them to analyze their learning styles, strengths, and weaknesses. Self-assessment encourages students to recognize patterns in their growth over time and set realistic goals for their learning.

> Clearly, learners know themselves better than anybody else. If we teachers include them as participants in the evaluation of their own learning, not only will they gain more control of their own study and development, but also we will have a better understanding of them as learners and as people. Learner-centered assessment should be considered a necessary part of student-centered instruction. (Fu, 1992, p. 183)

As teachers, you can gain valuable information when young people learn to articulate how and why they learn best. By encouraging and listening to students' self-reflections, you can make more effective judgments about what students have actually learned and make wiser instructional decisions. Assessment becomes a conversation, rather than a test.

How Do You Use Self-Evaluation Forms?

We have included several forms and techniques that will help students evaluate their own growth and learning in a variety of areas. As with all the forms in this book, we encourage you to experiment and adapt the forms to meet your students' needs and ages. It is important to realize that not everything in class warrants self-evaluation. If students begin to groan when you ask them to use one of these forms, it may be a clue that you are overdoing it!

Students need to develop the language necessary to talk about the process of learning. The forms you use or develop should only use language and concepts with which the students are familiar. For instance, the reading self-evaluation form only works if you have spent considerable time talking about reading strategies with your students.

Learning to step back and reflect on what and how you learn is a developmental skill that improves with age and practice. You can also discover much about how primary children learn from listening to children and observing them during actual reading and writing. Too many pencil and paper forms may become overwhelming. If used sparingly, the reading and writing self-evaluation forms in Chapters 7 and 8 can be used effectively with beginning writers and readers, particularly if you transcribe their responses.

How Do You Model Self-Reflection?

One way that Patti Kamber fosters self-reflection is through what she calls debriefing sessions. For example, literature circles in Patti's fifth grade are student-led. While the groups are meeting to discuss novels, Patti moves around the room with a clipboard jotting down notes and occasionally sitting in on a group. After the literature circles are over, she calls the students together and summarizes her observations, extending the students' awareness by raising questions, identifying patterns, and celebrating growth. Students then add comments about what worked well and how they are improving as listeners and considerate participants. This thoughtful debriefing time helps students assimilate metacognitive language and begin to think reflectively.

Examples of Self-Evaluation

We've included two samples of self-evaluation forms that one teacher used at the end of a literature circle on *My Side of the Mountain* (George, 1988). The fourth graders had all read the book and met in literature circles for discussions two or three times each week. Students kept a parallel journal in which they had to survive in another climate from the one described in the book. The teacher learned that one student was having difficulty focusing during group discussions and another student had trouble reading this particular genre. No matter how often we use forms like these, we are always pleased by the honesty of students and the accuracy of their self-evaluation.

Do Students Become Better at Self-Reflection over Time?

One way to provide support is to begin with questions or prompts that guide students as they begin to reflect on their learning. For instance, when Patti Kamber asks her fifth graders to complete a self-evaluation form, she begins with the question: "What did I do well today and/ or improve on during literature circles?" At the beginning of the year, the form includes a list of prompts that give students some scaffolding from which to build: asked good questions, helped someone else to understand something, listened empathetically, took a risk, tried to be open-minded, showed evidence, and compared something to real life. She discusses and spotlights each of these strategies when she observes them during literature circles. Once her students understand the concepts and have used the form for several months, Patti simply removes the prompts. Here are two students' responses in the spring:

> I had an intelligent discussion. I told my ideas for a minute and I listened well by looking straight into the speaker's eyes. Today our group took thinking time and that's a big change for us.

> I've gotten a lot better at talking since the beginning of the year because I don't lay low in the group and wait until somebody else says something similar to what I wanted to say. Instead, I say what I want to say, and sometimes it's a little too much and I get carried away.

The second question on the form is, "What do I still need to improve on during our literature circles?" The same two students answered:

> I need to get to the point because my group got a little bored. I guess I'm thinking while I'm talking instead of before I talk. Next time, I think I can get to the point by using my notes a little more. This can be tricky.

> I think I need to improve on not talking so much. I say what I want to say, but sometimes it's too much. I know this because they start looking around and flipping their pencils.

My Side of the Mountain Self-Evaluation

Name _____

Date _____

1 = poor
2 = fair
3 = OK
4 = good
5 = great

On a scale of 1–5, how would you evaluate yourself in these areas?

_____ Reading the book.
_____ Literature Circle discussions.
_____ Journal Writing project.

Write about all three parts of the literature circle project on My Side of the Mountain. What did you enjoy? What did you learn or improve in? What was hard for you? What would you do differently next time? What was the best part?

My Side of the Mountain Self-Evaluation

Name _____

Date _____

1 = poor
2 = fair
3 = OK
4 = good
5 = great

On a scale of 1–5, how would you evaluate yourself in these areas?

_____ Reading the book.
_____ Literature Circle discussions.
_____ Journal Writing project.

Write about all three parts of the literature circle project on My Side of the Mountain. What did you enjoy? What did you learn or improve in? What was hard for you? What would you do differently next time? What was the best part?

Don't you wish professors and presenters were so astute! Patti's questions and prompts reflect the goals of literature circles and her values.

To show how students acquire metacognitive language with modeling and practice, we've included an example of a debriefing form that Patti uses at other times. On the first form (page 169) you can see how the student answered briefly with rather meaningless phrases such as "OK" or "fine." The same child filled out the next form five months later. Note the increased length and richness of the responses and the depth of thought reflected in her answers. How wonderful it would be to hear and see more insights like Blair's: "I asked and asked until it was clear and I wasn't thinking about what I was going to say while someone else was talking."

Don't be discouraged if your students' responses are shallow at first. Many students (and adults) are not used to being asked these kinds of questions. We're all conditioned to having someone else evaluate us, however inadequately, rather than evaluating ourselves. Self-reflection is a valuable skill that will benefit students for the rest of their lives.

Self-reflection fosters independence in learners. Students learn to assess their own strengths and weaknesses, and to create meaningful goals for the future. As teachers, we should frequently remind ourselves that the primary goal of evaluation is to prepare and empower learners to evaluate themselves.

SELF-PORTRAITS

Self-portraits are simply pictures children draw of themselves. A child's portrait shows growth, much like a child's yearly school pictures. Developmental changes and growing artistic skill and perceptions are all reflected in the drawings a child does. If you ask the child to sign the portrait, you can also see changes in the child's writing skills and letter formation. When collected regularly, patterns begin to emerge. In addition, self-portraits are fun to look at side-by-side! You can precut paper to the size of the square, then mount the child's fall self-portrait next to the spring picture on the form provided on page 171.

INTEREST SURVEYS

An interest survey is a form used to discover a child's interests and hobbies, both in and out of school. The survey may be completed by the student or transcribed by a teacher or parent during an individual conference.

Why Use Interest Surveys?

Knowing a child's interests can help you guide children to books, suggest a writing topic, or get to know the child. The information from the interest survey will also help you know a child's depth of background knowledge about a variety of topics. The information from the interest survey could be shared with cross grade buddies or pen pals.

There are two forms on pages 173–175, beginning with a Personal Inventory that you may wish to keep in your Teacher's Notebook. The form for each child includes information about the child's home, friends, and interests. You may wish to fill out this form during the first conference you have with a student at the beginning of the year.

The Interest Survey is a form which older students could complete independently in September. You could ask primary students these questions and transcribe their answers onto the form.

Literature Circle Debriefing

Name_____Blair_____ Date___Oct 1_____

Title_____Sign of the Beaver_____ Author_____

My Group:

Today's discussion was_____fine_____

because___we all had our stuff_____

_____

_____

We could improve by_____talking more_____

_____

_____

Me:

My attitude in literature circles today was_____ok_____

because_____

_____

My participation was _____ok_____

because_____it was fine_____

I could improve by/if_____I asked a "why" question instead of a fact_____

_____

_____

_____

Literature Circle Debriefing

Name _Blair_   Date _May 1_

Title _Light in the Forest_   Author _Conrad Richter_

My Group:

Today's discussion was _alot better than yesterday_

because _yesterday the author totally confused us by jumping all around the plot. It was like talking about something with peanut butter on our brains._

We could improve by _Rereading confusing parts with our group or with you like we did yesterday. Now everyone wants to keep going but that was a close one._

Me:

My attitude in literature circles today was _definetely improved_

because _I think I figured out why the author wrote this and why we are reading it and it helped my attitude once understood what was happening._

My participation was _brilliant_

because _I kept asking questions until I finally figured out the problem. And I wasn't thinking about my point while someone else was talking_

I could improve by/if _I re-read slowly and take my Lit. circle home with me because when I get stuck there I have to wait 12 hrs. to have the problem cleared up._

Spring Self-Portrait

Fall Self-Portrait

Name: _____ Date: _____

Name: _____ Date: _____

Spring Self-Portrait

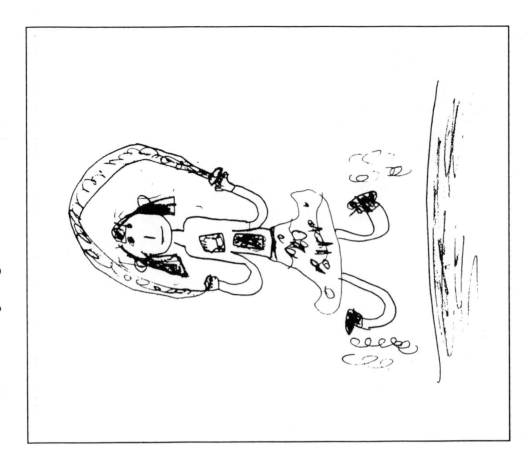

Name: _____ Date: _____

Fall Self-Portrait

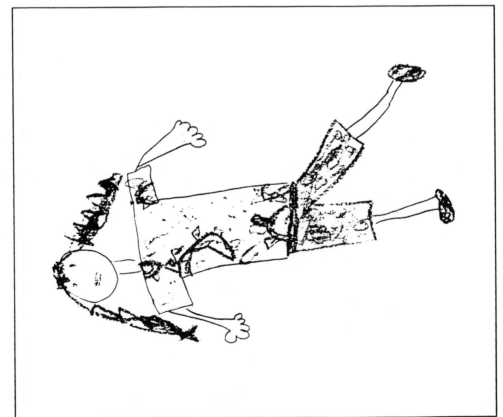

Name: _____ Date: _____

172

Personal Inventory of _____ **Birthdate** _____

Grade_____ Year_____ Interviewed by _____

SCHOOL PHOTO		The most important thing to know about me is:	
Who lives in your home? People? Pets?		Their occupations?	
Languages spoken at home?		My friends	
My interests: Sports Hobbies Clubs Lessons		My favorite: Book(s) Author(s)	
Places I've visited:		Things that have happened to me:	

Interest Survey

Name_____Grade_____Teacher_____Date_____

1. What kinds of things do you like to do outside of school?

_____

_____

_____

2. What organized activities do you do outside of school? (sports, clubs, lessons)

_____

_____

_____

3. What do you write about at home?

_____

_____

_____

4. What kinds of things do you like to read at home? (books, magazines, comics, newspapers)

_____

_____

_____

5. What do you like to read about?

_____

_____

_____

6. What do you want to be when you grow up?

_____

_____

_____

7. What are your parents' jobs? What kinds of things do they do at work?

_____

_____

_____

8. What is your favorite subject at school? Why? Least favorite? Why?

_____

_____

_____

9. What would you really like to learn about this year? Why?

_____

_____

_____

10. What's something about you that people at school might not know?

_____

_____

_____

11. Have you ever travelled? Where?

_____

_____

_____

12. What else would you like me to know about you?

_____

_____

_____

ATTITUDE SURVEYS

An attitude survey is an instrument used to find out about a student's general perceptions of school, or attitudes toward specific content areas. There are many published attitude surveys. Be sure to look at them closely; some are better than others. One hazard of using an attitude survey is that some children may give you the answers they think you want to hear rather than their honest opinion. Assure them there is no one right answer and that you really want their honest response, then observe students to see if their responses are supported by their behavior.

How Do Teachers Give an Attitude Survey?

The survey may be completed by the student or transcribed by a teacher or parent. Young children may give more thoughtful answers if an adult transcribes their responses. You may also want to develop an attitude survey which parents can complete at home, at parent night, or after conferences. We've included a Parent Survey in the next chapter on parent involvement in the assessment process.

Why Use an Attitude Survey?

Attitude plays an important part in the learning process. A positive attitude is necessary in order for students to become actively engaged in learning. Research shows that attitude and achievement are linked; therefore, we need to know how students feel about reading, writing, content areas, and learning in general in order to support student learning.

Reading and Writing Attitude Surveys

We've included several forms, ranging from very simple ones that younger children can complete, to longer forms that provide more detailed information. Be aware that sometimes when you ask students how they feel about writing, they may think you mean handwriting rather than composition!

The first set of forms on pages 177–180 focuses specifically on attitudes toward writing, reading, and spelling. The first two, the Student Writing Attitude Survey and Student Reading Attitude Survey, are parallel multiple-choice forms that can be easily used with younger students. Information from these forms is easy to compile to gain a general picture of your students' attitudes.

The next two parallel forms on pages 181–182 (Writing Attitude Survey and Reading Attitude Survey) are more open-ended and provide richer data. Adults can transcribe student responses for younger students and older students can complete these forms independently.

Writing and Reading Self-Evaluation Forms

We've included the next set of Writing and Reading Self-Evaluation forms on pages 183–187 to show how the same form can be adapted for different times in the year. Although they look alike at first glance, the first two forms solicit more general information about the student's attitudes and concepts about writing. You may want to use the next surveys at the end of each term to focus more on writing growth and goal setting. The final Writing Evaluation in this series encourages students to reflect on the writing they have done during the whole year.

⫽⫽⫽ Student Writing Attitude Survey ⫽⫽⫽

Name_____Age_____Date_____Teacher_____

A. I like to draw.

    not at all   a little   some   a lot   a whole lot

---

1. I like writing stories.

    not at all   a little   some   a lot   a whole lot

2. Writing is boring.

    not at all   a little   some   a lot   a whole lot

3. I like to write in my spare time.

    not at all   a little   some   a lot   a whole lot

4. I enjoy writing notes and letters to people.

    not at all   a little   some   a lot   a whole lot

5. I like writing at school.

    not at all   a little   some   a lot   a whole lot

6. I have trouble thinking about what to write.

    not at all   a little   some   a lot   a whole lot

7. It's fun to write things at home.

    not at all   a little   some   a lot   a whole lot

8. I like to share my writing with others.

    not at all   a little   some   a lot   a whole lot

---

9. Writing is fun.

    not at all   a little   some   a lot   a whole lot

10. I wish I had more time to write at school.

    not at all   a little   some   a lot   a whole lot

11. I like to read.

    not at all   a little   some   a lot   a whole lot

12. I think I'm a good writer.

    not at all   a little   some   a lot   a whole lot

13. I like to write.

    not at all   a little   some   a lot   a whole lot

14. How often do you write at home?

    not at all   a little   some   a lot   a whole lot

15. What kinds of things do you write? (types, topics or titles)

_____

_____

_____

_____

_____

_____

_____

_____

_____

_____

✑✑✑Student Reading Attitude Survey✑✑✑

Name_____Age_____ Date_____Teacher_____

A. I like to draw.

    not at all   a little   some   a lot   a whole lot

1. I like reading stories.

    not at all   a little   some   a lot   a whole lot

2. Reading is boring.

    not at all   a little   some   a lot   a whole lot

3. I like to read in my spare time.

    not at all   a little   some   a lot   a whole lot

4. I enjoy reading poetry.

    not at all   a little   some   a lot   a whole lot

5. I like reading at school.

    not at all   a little   some   a lot   a whole lot

6. I have trouble understanding what I read.

    not at all   a little   some   a lot   a whole lot

7. It's fun to read at home.

    not at all   a little   some   a lot   a whole lot

8. I enjoy talking about what I read.

    not at all   a little   some   a lot   a whole lot

9. Reading is fun.

    not at all   a little   some   a lot   a whole lot

10. I wish I had more time to read at school.

    not at all   a little   some   a lot   a whole lot

11. I like to read stories I have written.

    not at all   a little   some   a lot   a whole lot

12. I think I'm a good reader.

    not at all   a little   some   a lot   a whole lot

13. I like to read.

    not at all   a little   some   a lot   a whole lot

14. How often do you read at home?

    not at all   a little   some   a lot   a whole lot

15. What kinds of things do you read? (types, topics or titles)

_____

_____

_____

_____

_____

_____

_____

_____

_____

Writing Attitude Survey

Student's name_____Interviewer_____ Date_____

Directions: Ask the student the question and give him/her time to think. Prompt the child to give more detailed answers. Ask the child to explain why or give an example.

How do you feel about writing?_____
_____

When and how did you learn to write?_____
_____
_____

What kinds of things do you write at school?_____
_____
_____

What kinds of writing do you do at home?_____
_____
_____

Why do you think it's important to be a good writer?_____
_____
_____

How do you feel when you are asked to share your writing with others?_____
_____
_____

How do you feel when others share their writing with you?_____
_____
_____

How do you feel about yourself as a writer?_____
_____
_____

Reading Attitude Survey

Student's name_____Interviewer_____Date_____

Directions: Ask the student the question and give him/her time to think. Prompt the child to give more detailed answers. Ask the child to explain why or give an example.

How do you feel about reading?_____
_____

When and how did you learn to read?_____
_____
_____

What kinds of things do you like to read at school?_____
_____
_____

What kinds of things do you like to read at home?_____
_____
_____

Do you read to anyone in your family? Who? When? How do you feel about it?_____
_____
_____

Why do you think it's important to be a good reader?_____
_____
_____

How do you feel when your teacher reads aloud?_____
_____
_____

How do you feel when you read aloud to others at school?_____
_____

How do you feel when someone gives you a book for a present?_____
_____

How do you feel about yourself as a reader?_____
_____
_____

⟋⟋⟋Writing Self-Evaluation⟋⟋⟋

Name _____ Date _____

1. What makes a person a good writer?

   _____

   _____

   _____

2. Are you or are you not a good writer? Why do you think so?

   _____

   _____

   _____

3. Do you enjoy writing? Why or why not?

   _____

   _____

   _____

4. What kinds of writing do you most enjoy doing? Why?

   _____

   _____

   _____

5. What was the last thing you wrote outside of school? When? For whom
   and why did you write it?

   _____

   _____

   _____

◼◼◼Reading Self-Evaluation◼◼◼

Name _____ Date _____

1. What makes a person a good reader?

   _____

   _____

   _____

2. Are you or are you not a good reader? Why do you think so?

   _____

   _____

   _____

3. Do you enjoy reading? Why or why not?

   _____

   _____

   _____

4. What kind of reading do you most enjoy doing? Why?

   _____

   _____

   _____

5. What was the last thing you read outside of school? When?
   Why did you read it?

   _____

   _____

   _____

⫽⫽⫽Writing Self-Evaluation⫽⫽⫽

Name _____ Date _____

1. In what ways have you improved as a writer? What have you done well?

   _____

   _____

   _____

2. What writing have you most enjoyed during this term? Why?

   _____

   _____

   _____

3. Do you enjoy writing? Why or why not?

   _____

   _____

   _____

4. What things do you especially want to work on next term?

   _____

   _____

   _____

5. How often do you write outside of school? What was the last thing you wrote outside of school? Why did you write it?

   _____

   _____

   _____

   _____

◣◣◣Reading Self-Evaluation◣◣◣

Name _____ Date _____

1. In what ways have you improved as a reader? What have you done well?

   _____

   _____

   _____

2. What reading have you most enjoyed during this term? Why?

   _____

   _____

   _____

3. Do you enjoy reading? Why or why not?

   _____

   _____

   _____

4. What things do you especially want to work on next term?

   _____

   _____

   _____

5. How often do you read outside of school? What was the last thing you read
   outside of school? Why did you read it?

   _____

   _____

   _____

   _____

✐✐✐Writing Self-Evaluation✐✐✐

Name _____ Date _____

1. What is the best piece you have written this year? What makes it your best?

   _____

   _____

   _____

   _____

2. What are your strengths as a writer?

   _____

   _____

   _____

3. What do you need help with?

   _____

   _____

   _____

4. If you could change any piece in your Writer's Portfolio, which one would it be? What would you change about it?

   _____

   _____

   _____

   _____

5. Anything else?

   _____

   _____

   _____

   _____

SPELLING SURVEY

The next form in this section is the Spelling Survey. Students' responses could reveal valuable information about their attitudes toward spelling. The first question asks if students consider themselves good spellers. The questions on the form also ask children to articulate the spelling strategies they use while composing. Students are asked about strategies they use when they have trouble spelling a word. Many poor writers and spellers rely on one strategy, such as "sounding it out." Results from the survey can help you discover which strategies your students use. You may then want to model and discuss other techniques during your lessons.

MATH AND SCIENCE SURVEY

The Math Survey and Science Survey were designed to elicit information about students' attitudes toward these two particular content areas. Although it's important not to overwhelm your students with self-assessment forms and surveys, the information you gather can help you build on students' strengths and interest. Unfortunately, society still has a long way to go towards fostering a positive attitude and confidence about math and science among girls. Inviting guest speakers and reading about women in the sciences can help breakdown stereotypes. You may want to adapt the forms to use again at the end of the year.

Spelling Survey

Name_____ Date_____

1. Are you or are you not a good speller? Why do you think so?

   _____

   _____

   _____

2. What do you do when you don't know how to spell a word?

   _____

   _____

   _____

3. If someone is having trouble spelling a word, how could you help that person?

   _____

   _____

   _____

4. What three things help you learn to spell a new word?

   a. _____

   b. _____

   c. _____

5. What things have you tried that <u>do not</u> help your spelling?

   a. _____

   b. _____

   c. _____

   On the back, please add other comments you would like to share about spelling. You might include your feelings about spelling, how to choose words to study, how to practice, etc.

Math Survey

Name_____ Date_____

1. Do you enjoy math? Why or why not?

   _____

   _____

   _____

2. What helps someone become good at math?

   _____

   _____

   _____

3. Describe some ways in which people use math in "real life."

   _____

   _____

   _____

4. What types of math topics and activities do you most enjoy?

   _____

   _____

   _____

5. How have you used math outside of school?

   _____

   _____

   _____

6. Any other comments about math (feelings you have about math, types of math activities or topics you find difficult, etc.).

   _____

   _____

   _____

Science Survey

Name_____ Date_____

1. Do you consider yourself a scientist? Why or why not?

   _____

   _____

   _____

2. What helps someone become a good scientist?

   _____

   _____

   _____

3. Name several types of scientists.

   _____

   _____

   _____

4. Do you enjoy science? Why or why not?

   _____

   _____

   _____

5. What kinds of science do you most enjoy?

   _____

   _____

   _____

6. Describe any scientific experiments you've done or any science books you've read.

   _____

   _____

   _____

7. Any other comments about science (topics you'd like to study, feelings you have about science, etc.).

   _____

REFLECTION

It's important to know ourselves as learners. Many of us are unaware of some of our strengths and weaknesses until we are adults. On the next page is a form called Myself as a Learner that Carrie Holloway adapted from *Evaluating Literacy* (Anthony, et al., 1991). It can provide you with general information about how your students learn. In addition, the questions can encourage students to begin to think metacognitively about how they best learn and share ideas.

Asking Students to Reflect

The questions on the next group of forms help students to reflect on a specific assignment, their day, their week, or school in general. Although you would want to use these tools sparingly, the information from such forms could elicit surprising information and may help you better meet your student's needs.

You may decide to give the Student Attitude Survey (p. 194) at the beginning of the year to discover students' feelings about school in general. The Student Interview (page 195) and What I Learned About Myself forms (page 196) are more appropriate midyear, and provide helpful information to discuss at parent conferences. Teachers who have used the forms found they gained valuable information, particularly from quieter students who may hesitate to bring up concerns. Although these forms could have been included under the section on attitude surveys, we placed them here because they focus more generally on school, rather than on a particular area.

Weekly Review

The Weekly Review on page 197 is a pleasant way to reflect on the week's activities and help students set goals for the upcoming week. Parents enjoy receiving this each Friday. You may want to photocopy student responses periodically for your own records or student portfolios.

Myself as a Writer and Reader

The last form in this section can be used to compare children's perceptions of their literacy development over several years. The Myself as a Writer and Reader form contains only four questions to ask each student at the end of the year. You can record the child's responses in one column. The next year the student could be asked the same questions and the answers recorded in the next space. Students love to look back on their previous responses! This simple form is one more way of celebrating growth over time. You may wish to keep this form in the Learning Profile (Chapter 13) that follows students throughout their elementary years.

Myself as a Learner

Name _____ Date _____ Grade _____

Please circle the words YES, SOMETIMES, or NO to tell your feelings about each of these statements about learning:

1. I wonder about things and like to find out about them.	YES	SOMETIMES	NO
2. I like to read on my own. I like books and read a lot.	YES	SOMETIMES	NO
3. I like other people to read to me.	YES	SOMETIMES	NO
4. I like to share my ideas by talking.	YES	SOMETIMES	NO
5. I like to share my ideas by acting things out.	YES	SOMETIMES	NO
6. I like to share my ideas by drawing.	YES	SOMETIMES	NO
7. I like to share my ideas by writing.	YES	SOMETIMES	NO
8. I keep working at things even if they seem hard	YES	SOMETIMES	NO
9. When I'm reading or writing and I don't know a word, I try to figure it out myself and keep on going.	YES	SOMETIMES	NO

Use your words to finish these comments:

I especially like to read, write, and learn about _____

I am really good at _____

One thing that I find difficult is _____

Anything else? _____

Student Attitude Survey

Name_____ Grade_____ Teacher_____Date_____

1. What do you like about school? Why?

_____

_____

2. What don't you like about school? Why?

_____

_____

3. What is the easiest thing for you at school? Why?

_____

_____

4. What is the hardest thing for you at school?

_____

_____

5. What do you think would make this easier for you?

_____

_____

6. What accomplishment are you most proud of here at school? Why?

_____

_____

7. What do you want to learn about next?

_____

_____

8. Is there anything else you'd like to say about your feelings about school?

_____

_____

STUDENT INTERVIEW

Name_____

What do you like about being in our class? Why?

_____

_____

If you could change something at school, what would that be? Why?

_____

_____

What do you find the easiest? Why is this easy for you?

_____

_____

What do you find difficult? Why is this difficult for you?

_____

_____

Who do you like to work with in class? Why?

_____

_____

Who do you like to play with at recess? What do you like to do?

_____

_____

Is there anyone you have trouble getting along with? Why?

_____

_____

What are you especially proud about learning this term?

_____

_____

What would you like to learn about next?

_____

_____

What do you think is important to say about you in the conference (or on the progress report)?

_____

_____

Please use the back to include anything else you want me to know.

What I Learned About Myself

This year,

1. I think I have improved in:

a._____

b._____

c._____

2. I was happy when_____

_____

3. I still need to work on_____

_____

4. If I could change one thing about myself, it would be_____

_____

_____

5. This year I learned how to_____

_____

6. One new thing I discovered about myself was

_____

_____

_____

Weekly Review

Name_____ Date _____

1. What was your biggest achievement this week?

_____

_____

_____

2. What was your favorite activity this week? Why?

_____

_____

_____

3. In what area did you improve the most? What improvement(s) did you make?

_____

_____

_____

4. In what area do you feel the need for the most help?

_____

_____

_____

5. Write one goal for next week and tell how you plan to reach it.

_____

_____

_____

_____

_____

_____

MYSELF AS A WRITER AND READER

Name _____

Teacher:	Teacher:	Teacher:
Date:	Date:	Date:
What have you learned recently as an author?	What have you learned recently as an author?	What have you learned recently as an author?
What would you like to learn to become a better writer?	What would you like to learn to become a better writer?	What would you like to learn to become a better writer?
What have you learned recently in reading?	What have you learned recently in reading?	What have you learned recently in reading?
What would you like to learn to become a better reader?	What would you like to learn to become a better reader?	What would you like to learn to become a better reader?

TEACHER EVALUATIONS

As teachers, we also need to assess our own learning and professional progress. At some point in your career, some of you may remember teacher evaluations based on a thirty-minute observations based on an I.T.I.P. checklist. How much more meaningful it would have been to have shared your professional portfolio with your supervisor. Across the country, teachers are beginning to keep their own portfolios alongside their students. Teacher portfolios can contain personal information, professional writing, pictures of activities in your classroom, and letters from parents. You may wish to include logs of books you've read and reflections about your teaching and professional growth. The process of keeping your own portfolio will provide valuable insights. In his work with teachers, Donald Graves (1993) commented, "Maintaining our own portfolios has contributed more to our understanding of the possibilities and use than virtually any other aspect of our work with them" (p. 5).

Carrie Holloway designed the previous form, What I Learned About Myself, as a final reflection for her students at the end of the year. We've found the form works equally well with graduate students and adults. We've also developed a form called, My Teacher's Report Card, based on the process described in *Evaluating Literacy* (1991), which students could use to evaluate you! If you've fostered a positive classroom environment and genuinely want to improve your own teaching, the responses could be very helpful. The last form is a self-evaluation for you as a teacher. The Teacher Self-Evaluation could become part of your supervisor's review and could be included in your personal portfolio. We feel it's very important for both students and teachers to step back and reflect on and celebrate their hard work and growth.

My Teacher's Report Card

Name of Teacher _____ Name of Student_____

Directions: Please evaluate your teacher using the following system.
Use the comment section to explain or give examples.

1 - Great
2 - Good
3 - Okay
4 - Needs Improvement

Score	Area	Comments
☐	Friendliness	_____
☐	Fairness	_____
☐	Teaching	_____
☐	Explaining	_____
☐	Encouraging	_____
☐	Listening	_____
☐	Sense of Humor	_____

Teacher Self-Evaluation

Looking back on this year, some of the things I feel best about are

_____

_____

Looking back at my goals in September,_____

_____

_____

The parts of my curriculum about which I feel best are

_____

_____

_____

_____

The aspects of my teaching about which I feel best are _____

_____

_____

_____

The hardest things for me this year were _____

_____

_____

I learned _____

_____

_____

Two of my goals for next year are _____

_____

_____

Over the summer I hope to _____

_____

_____

CHAPTER ELEVEN

Involving Parents
in Assessment

D o you have school age children? Do you remember the first parent conference when you were sitting on the other side of the desk? It can be a humbling and enlightening experience! Parents want to hear that we care about their child and know him or her as a wonderful, unique individual. If we truly believe in teaching the whole child, it's important to share what we know with parents and to listen to what they have to share.

INVOLVING PARENTS IN ASSESSMENT

Traditionally, families have been left outside the assessment process, yet parents are the ones who know their children best. In this chapter we will talk about the role of parents. We recognize, however, that in some homes, the primary care-givers may be foster parents, grandparents, siblings, or other relatives. When you ask family members to reflect, respond, and contribute in the assessment process, you acknowledge that education is a shared responsibility between home and school. You also signal that you value parents' perspectives. In this chapter we describe a few avenues for encouraging parents to become involved in the assessment and evaluation process.

When we give parents the opportunity to assess their child's learning, they become more aware of *what* to observe and *how* their child learns. You can then sit, side by side, and share your own insights with families. These discussions also become a vehicle for you to explain your philosophy and curriculum. In return, the information you glean from parents can provide valuable clues about how to best meet the needs of each student.

The more that you depart from traditional curriculum, testing, and report cards, the greater the need to communicate with parents. Families are generally very supportive once you articulate your rationale for change. It's important that you explain that your changes are soundly based on current research and provide a deeper understanding of their child as a learner.

Parent Survey

At the beginning of the year, a parent survey can provide a wealth of information about each student. The Parent Survey (page 205) and My Child As a Learner (page 206–207) forms include questions about a child's attitudes and literacy behaviors at home. Space is provided for parents to note a child's strengths and interests. These two forms are most appropriate to use at the beginning of the year. You might want to have parents complete one of these forms before fall parent conferences. The Family Questionnaire (page 208) would be more applicable later in the year. It's interesting to discover when a child's behavior is different at home than it is at school. You can discover facts about children and their families that will sometimes give you a glimpse of their lives outside the classroom.

OTHER WAYS TO INVOLVE PARENTS

One way to involve parents is to encourage them to help in the classroom. Seeing their child in daily school activities is often enlightening and gives parents a sense of what happens in your room. You can invite parent help in the classroom or on field trips. It's important to make families feel welcome. At Back to School Night, you may also want to invite parents to share their favorite children's book sometime during the year as "guest reader." The more welcome you make parents feel, the more open the lines of communication become.

Parent Observations

When parents come to visit, it's helpful for them to be able to step back and observe their child "in action." Parents usually hear only bits and snatches of what goes on at school and often relish seeing how their child interacts in the classroom. The *Primary Program Resource Document* (1992) from British Columbia has a wonderful section on parent observations. Based on their work and our own experience, we developed a Parent Observation Guide (page 209) that can help structure a parent's observations and discussion afterwards.

Parent Conferences

In some schools, conferences have become three-way conversations between parents, students, and teachers. The student shares his or her portfolio and leads the discussion. In order for student-led conferences to be successful, you must do a great deal of advance planning with your students. The *Primary Program Resource Document* by the Ministry of Education in British Columbia, Canada, (1992) and *Evaluating Literacy* (Anthony, et al., 1991) describe student-led conferences. Some teachers on Bainbridge Island have just begun student-led conferences and are adapting their forms from the B.C. documents. One problem that has quickly become evident is that twenty-minute parent conferences are not long enough for teachers to explain the continuum and progress reports, and for students to share their portfolios. As assessment and evaluation change, schools may need to explore alternate methods for reporting.

In Chapter 6 on Emergent Readers and Writers, we described Jan Colby's process of meeting with individual students each trimester to write down observations about writing growth. We've included Jan's "We Noticed" form on page 210 as an example of how you can solicit parent input at conference time. At the parent conference, the student shares writing samples and the information on the form. The parents then add comments, and the form is stored in the student's portfolio. You may wish to adapt the process and form to address reading growth.

Phone Calls

We couldn't resist mentioning the incredible power of positive phone calls and notes. Take a few minutes each week to call or write one or two parents to let them know how much you're enjoying their child, something wonderful she or he did that day, or to share a breakthrough in reading or writing. When you call a parent, most expect you to be calling about a problem. To get a phone call or note celebrating something positive can absolutely flabbergast parents. You'll be amazed at the response!

Home Visits

Some of your students may have a single, working mother or father, parents who work late shifts or long hours, or parents who have had negative experiences with school. Those are often

Primary Parent Survey

Child's Name_____   Date_____

Please take a few minutes to reflect upon the growth of your child. Using the codes below, circle the numbers that best indicate your observations. Then complete the statements that follow and return this form to school.

1 = Most of the time
2 = Sometimes
3 = Rarely
4 = Never observed

My child:

	1	2	3	4
can stay on a task until completion	1	2	3	4
seems to want to learn/is curious about things	1	2	3	4
makes choices independently about using free time	1	2	3	4
chooses activities that entertain him/her (videos, Nintendo, etc.)	1	2	3	4
likes to draw or color	1	2	3	4
uses her/his own spelling	1	2	3	4
likes to write	1	2	3	4
likes to talk about or share his/her writing	1	2	3	4
likes to listen to family members read to her/him	1	2	3	4
tries to read in everyday situations (signs, labels, etc.)	1	2	3	4
tries to figure out new words for him/herself when reading	1	2	3	4
likes to read to others	1	2	3	4

My child seems to have a _____ attention span.
(long, average, short)

These are some of my child's strengths that I see: _____

_____

_____

Some of my child's interests are _____

_____

_____

Some areas where my child needs to improve are _____

_____

_____

**Please use the back of this form to write any concerns and/or questions you may have.
Thank you for your help!**

My Child as a Learner

Child's Name_____ Date _____

Parent(s) _____

**Since you are your child's first and best teacher,
we would like your perceptions of your child as a learner.
Thank you for your help!**

How does your child seem to feel about going to school?

_____

_____

_____

What are your goals for your child this year?

_____

_____

_____

What are your child's interests? (art, sports, lessons, pastimes)

_____

_____

_____

_____

_____

What types of activities do you do together as a family?

_____

_____

_____

_____

Do you have a time you read together regularly? If so, when and how often?

_____

_____

What types of books does your child enjoy? Any favorites?

_____

_____

Does your child discuss or retell stories you have read aloud?

_____

_____

What types of writing does your child do at home?

_____

_____

What are your observations about how your child learns?

_____

_____

What are some other things you would like me to know about your child?

_____

_____

_____

_____

_____

_____

_____

_____

_____

Family Questionnaire

Child's Name_____   Date _____

Please take a few moments to sit down with your child to complete
this form.   Your thoughtful ideas and opinions will help us
greatly in evaluating the success of our school program.

What is your response to how each of these areas have been addressed in our program?

AREA	RATING High............Low	ANY ADDITIONAL SPECIFIC COMMENTS?
Reading	1 2 3	_____
Writing	1 2 3	_____
Spelling	1 2 3	_____
Math	1 2 3	_____
Social Studies	1 2 3	_____
Science	1 2 3	_____
Field Trips	1 2 3	_____
Other:	1 2 3	_____
Other: _____	1 2 3	_____

Please describe your child's feelings toward school.

_____

_____

What are some school activities your child likes?   dislikes?

_____   _____

_____   _____

_____   _____

What changes have you noticed in your child since school began?

_____

_____

_____

**Please use the back of this form for your additional ideas, thoughts, concerns.
Thank you for your honest feedback.**

Parent Observation Guide

Date_____   Child's Name_____

Welcome to our classroom. You may want to take a few notes on what you observe your child doing while working alone, with me, or with other children. Use these prompts to guide you. We can discuss them later if you like. Enjoy your visit!

When I observed my child in the classroom today:

I noticed that s/he can_____

_____

_____

_____

I noticed my child especially enjoyed working on_____

_____

_____

_____

I wondered about_____

_____

_____

_____

After observing my child in class today:

I'd like to know _____

_____

_____

_____

I'd like to discuss the following goal(s) _____

_____

_____

_____

We Noticed...

Child's Name _____ Date_____

Title(s) of piece(s) of writing I chose:

_____

_____

What my teacher and I noticed I did well:

_____

_____

_____

_____

My goals for next time:

_____

_____

_____

Parent(s) response to this writing:

_____

_____

_____

_____

the parents who do not come to parent conferences. Sometimes a home visit can be a thoughtful way of showing that you care. One teacher used to visit all her kindergarten students in the summer before school began. It was amazing how much those 10-minute visits lessened the anxiety of the five-year-olds and opened the door to communication with families.

Another second-grade teacher visits her students at home once during the year. She first sends home a letter explaining that she would like to visit the child . . . not inspect housekeeping or confer with parents. She visits for only 15 minutes and plays whatever game the child wants. Parents are usually touched and the children are ecstatic. Those 15 minutes in each child's house provide a wealth of information about the child and his/her family. For many of those children, the teacher's visit is a turning point in their behavior at school. Although 25 or 30 home visits are very time-consuming, they provide great insight into children's home environments. You may want to begin by visiting just the children about whom you are concerned, then visit others if you have time.

Parent Letters

At the beginning of the year, many teachers send home a parent letter explaining their philosophy and program. The challenge is to keep your letter to one page, avoid jargon or talking down to parents, and convey a sense of enthusiasm. It's harder to do than it might seem. Some teachers have ended up designing a series of three or four letters, focusing on specific areas of the curriculum on the next page. We've included Carrie Holloway's parent letter about the writing program in her second-grade classroom.

CELEBRATING WITH FAMILIES

In Chapter 4 we described how Patti Kamber uses portfolios as a vehicle for ongoing communication between school and home. The students in Patti's classroom collect their work in a Friday Folder that they take home every two weeks, accompanied by a letter to their parents. The parent comments are shared with the teacher, then the students transfer their work into the filing cabinet for storage or into their portfolios. This ongoing dialogue between parents, the teacher, and students helps encourage communication and enables parents to see their child's work on a regular basis.

Patti also has regular Authors' Nights and Portfolio Nights. We've learned, especially with young students, to keep the sharing time under one or two hours. The Author's Night is far more pleasant when the children practice enough so they can read their piece smoothly. It's embarrassing for everyone to listen to a child mumble or stumble through a reading. Authors enjoy calling on one or two people in the audience for positive comments after sharing their writing.

Randi Ivancich, a first-grade teacher, publishes student writing with a library pocket so that other children can check out student books to read at home. Her students include an "All About the Author" page and several blank pages at the back where families can write positive responses to the author.

A third-grade teacher, Alice Mendoza, has a weekly Friday Poetry Recital. Students practice poems all week and then on Fridays, after lunch, gather chairs in a circle. Although students often begin with Shel Silverstein poems, by midyear they are reading a wider variety of poems, including ones that they have written themselves. Parents come to share favorite poems as well. The last Friday of every month includes both musical contributions and poetry. The Poetry Recital takes about an hour. Alice and her students spend the last part of the hour evaluating the recital. They note good inflection, projection, use of props, increasing level of challenge, and general impressions. Alice is often overwhelmed by students' honesty and their sincere recognition of each other's strengths and growth. She videotapes the weekly

Poetry Recital so students can take the tape home to share with families who can't attend. When the tape comes back, Alice reads the families' comments aloud and the tape circulates through the class.

September 8, 1993

Dear Parents,

I would like to share my goals for writing this year and let you know about the writing the students in our classroom will do each day. Also, I invite you to participate in your child's growth as a writer. Writing is important because it extends students' creative thinking and helps develop their ability to problem solve. It is a valuable life skill.

My primary goal for writing is to have students learn to look at their own writing and that of their peers to celebrate growth and decide how to improve.

Writing is a process that involves these overlapping stages:

Gathering Ideas In this step, children choose a topic. We will brainstorm ideas in class and I will encourage writers to look for stories and poems all the time in their everyday lives.

Drafting In this stage, children put their ideas on paper. I tell them nothing is permanent, and spelling and neatness are not uppermost at this stage.

Revision At this stage, children take a second look at what they have written. They should read with an audience in mind to make sure their writing makes sense. Some of the students' writing will end at this stage.

Editing This is fine-tuning. Students who are developmentally ready for this will work on the spelling and punctuation at this stage. They choose which pieces to edit.

Publishing If students have completed all of the stages listed above, they may choose to publish their work.

Each day we will devote about an hour to writing. This writing time is called "Writing Workshop." The Writing Workshop consists of these four elements:

Mini-Lessons The purpose of this short, whole-class lesson will be to present the skills of writing and mechanics in the context of the student's writing.

Writing Time The students will spend 30-40 minutes each day writing. Most often, students will pick their own topics. They will also decide if they want to continue a piece, or start something new. They will keep ongoing work in writing folders.

Conferences Within the writing time, students may choose to confer with peers or with the teacher. The purpose of writing conferences is to have writers receive feedback before they are done writing. The first conferences will focus on content; the last will address mechanics.

Group Sharing The last part of Writing Workshop will be a class sharing time. Students will be given the opportunity to read their in-process or finished work to receive feedback from their peers.

You can help your children develop as writers. First of all, let your children see you write and encourage them to participate. This might be through letters, shopping lists, or notes. You might want to try writing some stories, poems, or songs to share with your children. Also, since writing and reading are closely related, I encourage you to read with your children. Help them find information about their favorite authors.

I hope this letter has given you insights into writing in our classroom. If you have any questions, feel free to call me at school.

Sincerely,

Carrie Holloway

STRENGTHENING THE HOME-SCHOOL CONNECTION

Roz Duthie has developed a different type of ongoing communication with her kindergarten families. Rad Rabbit and Rad Raccoon (for the respective morning and afternoon classes) travel home with one child each night. Rad travels in a backpack with a notebook and pencil so that families can record what Rad did while visiting overnight. Roz says the idea has been incredibly successful as families record the everyday activities of five- and six-year-olds. At Halloween, Rad Rabbit came back to school wearing a custom-made witch hat, cape, and tiny broom. The fun continued and soon many kindergarteners began doing their own writing. No matter how busy, students never forget to remind Roz to read about Rad's adventures the night before and decide where Rad will travel next.

Jan Colby also has a class backpack that travels home with her kindergartners. In the backpack, Jan includes two books by the same author, a spiral journal, and a stuffed animal or artifact to go with the book. She staples a letter to the parents on the front cover of the journal encouraging families to share the books together at a comfortable, cozy, unhurried time. She suggests they talk about how the books are alike or different, what they like best, what they learned, etc. Jan recommends that parents help the children respond by taking dictation, helping children write or draw their responses. Parents like to add their own reactions to the books.

Jan asks parents to be observant as they read together. She asks a series of questions: Do the children know how to hold the book correctly? Did they grasp the content of the books? Could the children retell the story? Could they predict what might happen next? Are they attentive? Did they recognize any letters/sounds/words? Jan asks parents to record any observations they made while reading together. She suggests that parents not stop the flow of reading to "teach" these things, but to *observe* their child's progress the way she does at school. Jan's students love bringing the backpack back to school and enjoy sharing their responses. Parents are enthusiastic and students clamor to be the next to take the books home.

Mem Fox (1993), in her poignant writing, describes the power of the relationship between a child, an adult, and a book. The magic that occurs when families read together lays a strong foundation for literacy. "I'm certain that learning to read and learning to love reading owe a great deal (much more than we ever dreamed) to the *nature of the human relationships* that occur around and through books" (p. 136).

Although the activities described here are not specifically assessment tools, we included them as examples of ways to increase the connection between home and school. Regular opportunities for families to communicate with teachers help bridge the gap between home and school.

CHAPTER TWELVE

Involving Special Students in Assessment

A uthentic assessment is not just for "regular classrooms" or certain students. Authentic assessment provides a valid and reliable way of collecting, evaluating, and sharing what we know about all students, whether they are considered "gifted," "learning disabled," or "average." Rather than labeling children, we should focus on improving our teaching so we can meet the needs of every child.

In this chapter, we will use the term "specialists" to refer to Chapter I, ESL, CDS, Resource Room, or LAP teachers, or any professional other than the classroom teacher who works with special needs students.

ASSESSING SPECIAL STUDENTS

Most specialists have a strong commitment to working closely with classroom teachers. In some districts, faculties are examining new ways of scheduling and providing services to students with special needs. For instance, some specialists have begun to work with students in the classroom rather than working individually or in small groups in a Resource or Chapter I Room. So much depends on teachers, individual students, and the support of administrators. Our goal in this chapter is not to argue whether one program or approach is better than another, but to look at how we can best meet the needs of each student.

Assessment and evaluation, especially in special education, have traditionally focused on standardized testing with grade level equivalents and an emphasis on what children could not do. Tests are often mandated for program and state funding. The results from standardized tests were seldom useful for program planning or instruction. Teachers were often so busy testing and teaching that they failed to step back and observe and validate what children *could* do. You may not be able to affect the mandate to use standardized tests. However, you can at least supplement test results with three other valuable sources of information: observations, work samples, and asking children to reflect on their own learning.

Observations

Day to day observations are probably the most valuable pieces of information you can collect. You can observe children as they work with specialists and in the regular classroom. It's important to take the time to watch and listen to students.

One advantage to having specialists work in the classroom is that they can observe particular children in the busy context of the regular classroom. Specialists in the room can also free you to observe students, while they read to the class, present a mini-lesson, or teach a small group. Ongoing assessment from a variety of perspectives is invaluable.

Work Samples

You can also learn a great deal by looking at students' work. Specialists often have the advantage of working with individual students or small groups. Slowing down, clarifying misconceptions, providing individual instruction, and explaining strategies and concepts can be a great help to students. Specialists can also gather more time-consuming and specific diagnostic information such as more frequent running records or a miscue analysis.

You must keep in mind, however, that the samples you collect only capture a slice of the child's learning. Jan Peacoe is a special education teacher on Bainbridge Island. While reading *Mossflower* (Jacques, 1988) to a student, Jan looked over and saw another child with paper and pencil in front of him, staring off into space. Thinking his mind was at recess or elsewhere, she gently, but firmly asked him to get back to work. He said, defensively, "But I am working! Do you want to hear what I am doing? I'm listening to you read and noticing how the author is describing that scene. I'm trying to figure out how I can use words like that in my story." A great portion of learning is underground and invisible; how lucky we are when we catch glimpses of children's connections and insights.

Talking with Students

You can gather rich information whenever you talk with students. Specialists often have the luxury of working with the same student for several years and can develop a special caring relationship. By asking students their opinions, teachers can empower students with the confidence they may lack in themselves as learners in a system that has labeled them as "disabled" or different. Talking with them about both what and how they are learning, can give you insights into how to best support their learning. Listening gives you clues about the dreams and aspirations of these learners.

For example, Jan Peacoe was continually trying to encourage Tim to write when all he wanted to do was to draw. After months, this first grader obliged by writing stories to accompany his drawings; however, his enthusiasm was lacking. When Jan asked Tim to select a piece for his portfolio, she was sure he'd choose a wonderful fishing story he had written. Instead, he selected a piece with very little text but a colorful, elaborate picture. When Jan asked why he chose that piece, he said proudly, "Well, just look at how I filled up the whole picture space with lots of colors. My drawing is great and it tells the story." At that point Jan thought about all the wonderful picture books she had shared with Tim. She began to validate what was important to Tim and to all her students. Once she listened to Tim's stories and praised him for his growth as an illustrator, he began to blossom as a writer.

One way to discover children's interests is to give them an Interest Inventory or Attitude Survey (Chapter 10). The challenge is finding time to meet together to share discoveries and insights!

In the first article in *With Promise* (1991), Alfreda Furnas, a special education teacher says,

> Mostly, I ask myself, does this child feel good about himself as a reader, writer, learner? Does this child feel successful? Does this child see reading and writing as a joy, not a task? If I can answer yes to these questions, I know that the child is making progress, no matter how subtle. (p. 7)

Your job as a teacher is to observe, document, and celebrate the growth in each child's fluency and confidence. To best meet the needs of individual children, it's important to learn what types of classroom conditions are available to support children in their quest for literacy.

THE COMPONENTS OF THE READING/WRITING CURRICULUM FORM

In the last few years, the Bainbridge Island School District has moved toward a whole language curriculum. The Components of the Reading/Writing Curriculum form (pages 218–219) was developed, based on the district's language arts curriculum, to help specialists discover what types of learning and instruction exist in each classroom.

It's important to stress that this form is not used to evaluate teachers. In some schools and with some teachers, the form may be too intimidating or make teachers feel uncomfortable. Specialists may want to begin by using this form with teachers who are already comfortable with whole language. This form will provide a very specific picture of the types of activities in each classroom. Teachers are all at different stages of professional growth and it's important to recognize that each teacher develops their own areas of strength and expertise.

Your goal should be to ascertain the types of teaching and learning that occur in each classroom, in order to support or supplement learning for special students. For example, a Chapter I teacher might want to go into a classroom to work with a student during literature circles. The same teacher may help another child by reading the book aloud which the class will be discussing. Students could also come to the Chapter I Room to listen to a tape of the book before the literature circles meet.

THE SPECIAL SERVICES SCHEDULING SURVEY

The purpose of the Special Services Scheduling Survey (pages 220) is to determine what environment is most suited to each individual child, based on that child's needs. Each spring, the teachers complete the form for each student who receives special services. You can adapt the form to use with students who have been placed in a developmental kindergarten, Chapter I, ESL, Resource Room, or a Highly Capable/Gifted Program.

The first half of the form describes a continuum of services. In the first option, the student remains in the regular classroom and the Resource Room teacher serves as a consultant. At the other end of the continuum, most of the student's instruction occurs in the Resource Room. This form is divided into three sections (reading, writing, and math). By matching information about the child, the classroom components, and the teacher, specialists can decide whether they can be most effective working with each child in the regular classroom or in a separate environment.

The climate in the classroom is just as important as the types of activities and approaches. Is there a feeling of acceptance, respect, and encouragement for risk-taking? The goal should be to nourish each child's strengths and provide support for his/her areas for growth in the best possible environment. The surveys included in this chapter were developed to help place each child in the "least restrictive environment" in order to best meet his or her needs.

As schools move toward whole language, staff members may reexamine the role of specialists. In most schools, scheduling is a major concern and flexibility is the key. When a Resource Room or Chapter I teacher sees 30 or more students, it simply may not be possible to work in each individual classroom. Your staff may decide to group students with special needs so the specialist can work in fewer classrooms. Specialists may decide to rotate between working with students in the Resource Room and working in the classroom. So much depends on the individual child and the types of units or activities going on in the classroom. If these two forms are completed in the spring, specialists and teachers can work together to tackle the challenging issue of placement and scheduling for the next year. These changes can only occur in a supportive environment. Administrative and staff support are essential ingredients for making changes. As we've said throughout this book, it's important to start slowly. Change takes time!

Components of a Reading/Writing Curriculum

Teacher's Name _____ School _____ Grade _____

Listed below are possible components to the reading/writing curriculum.   It's unlikely that anyone does all of these, so please check only those you do in your classroom on a _regular_ basis.

_____ Writer's workshop: daily extended time period for writing

_____ Writer's Notebook: on-going collection of ideas, personal or exploratory writing

_____ Writer's /Author's Folder: contains current and past writing pieces

_____ Writing Conferences: one-to-one meetings on a regular basis with each child to evaluate and
                     discuss student's writing and provide specific instruction.

_____ Editing Checklist: list of self-checks for editing

_____ Editor's Table: place where peers help edit writing in preparation for publishing

_____ Publishing Center: materials for publishing writing

_____ Author's Circle: children share writing in process for peer feedback

_____ Author's Chair: children read finished pieces to audience and receive feedback

_____ Group Composed Books: students work cooperatively to create a shared writing piece

_____ Mini-lessons: brief lessons on reading/writing strategies and techniques

_____ Read Aloud: teacher reads books aloud on a daily basis

_____ Quiet Reading: daily extended time for quiet reading, sometimes called D.E.A.R. or S.S.R.

_____ Reading Conferences: one-to-one meetings on a regular basis with each child to evaluate and
                     discuss student's reading and provide specific instruction.

_____ Reading Logs: forms for students to record books read

_____ Dialogue/Response Journals: journal for written responses to literature

_____ Literature Circles: children meet in small groups on a regular basis to discuss books they
                     have read in common

_____ Reader's Theatre: students take on "parts" and informally act out a story they have read

_____ Learning Logs: notebook(s) for writing about learning in content areas

_____ Portfolios: on-going systematic collections of students' work and self-reflections

Please list other components which are a part of your language arts program. Add any which were not included as well as any other information which you feel is important about your classroom program.

_____ Core Books:

_____

_____

_____

_____

_____

_____

_____ Theme(s):

_____

_____

_____

_____ Class Projects (Island Reports, Book Company, etc.)

_____

_____

_____

_____ Other: (Author Focus, Pen Pal Projects, Doing Words, etc.)

_____

_____

_____

_____

_____

_____

Special Services Scheduling Survey

Student_____ Teacher _____ Date _____

	Reading	Math	Writing
1. Student will fully participate in regular classroom without any Special Services support (specially designed instruction).			
2. Student will fully participate in regular classroom with direct Special Services support (Specialist staff in regular classroom).			
3. A combination of 2 and 4 (student may receive support in classroom some of the time and receive services out of the classroom sometimes).			
4. Student will fully participate in regular classroom with supplementary support outside of classroom (student brings regular classroom materials).			
5. Student will work at a program similar to that in the regular classroom, but conducted entirely out of classroom by Special Services staff).			

Specific areas of concern:

_____

_____

_____

_____

_____

_____

_____

_____ YES   If there were a mixed-grade Writer's Workshop in the Resource Room,

_____ NO   would this student be a good candidate for that group?

Check any Special Services currently received by the student :

_____Developmental K   _____Chapter I   _____ESL   _____Resource Room   _____Highly Capable

What is your "best guess" as to the times these subjects will fit into your classroom schedule for this student? (e.g. from 10:00 to 10:45)	Reading _____ Math _____ Writing _____

_____ YES   Would you be willing to have within your class a small group of students who
_____ NO   require similar Special Services, if a member of the appropriate Special Services
staff was scheduled to be in your room for the part of each day when students
would need support?

USING THE ASSESSMENT FORMS WITH SPECIAL STUDENTS

Most of the forms in this book can be used with any student. Teachers or specialists may wish to transcribe responses for beginning writers or children for whom writing is difficult so students can concentrate on their ideas. Both classroom teachers and specialists can observe, take anecdotal notes, and collect work samples.

Once a week Jan Peacoe asks her students to write a response to something they read that week in the Resource Room or in their regular classroom. Children save their weekly responses and bind them into a book, along with a copy of their Reading Log (Chapter 8). The writing samples on the next pages from September, February, and April showed a record of Pete's growth in both reading and writing. Note the growth in length, complexity of ideas, spelling skills, and confidence. The first sample consists of two sentences: "This is a crab. I like crabs because my favorite color is red."

Five months later, Pete uses capitals and periods, correct spacing between words, and spells many words conventionally. In addition, the tone matches the task and provides an accurate summary of the book. Notice the remarkable change in Pete's drawing, including the shadow of the soccer ball. Pete wrote: "Soccer. I like soccer. I just read a book about soccer. A boy throws a ball through the window. The ball flew through the house and hit almost everything in the house."

The sample from February is one of three pages Pete wrote in response to a book. Perhaps because he was focusing on meaning, Pete doesn't use capitals and punctuation correctly in this piece. As a teacher, you might want to see other samples or ask him about the change. You may decide to ask him to do a second draft of this entry to include in his portfolio. The final sample is more complex in sentence structure, vocabulary, and use of detail. You can also see by these samples that Pete is reading longer and more challenging books. These samples clearly document Pete's growth as a reader and writer.

How Can Evaluation "Work" with Students in Special Programs?

Specialists may want to work together with teachers who are beginning to use portfolios to provide special students with additional time and support. Will students bring work from the Resource Room to add to their classroom portfolio? Specialists can help students write self-reflections about portfolio pieces and help students organize components. If the classroom teacher is not yet using portfolios, would students keep a portfolio in the Enrichment Program or Resource Room? Can students share writing from the classroom at Author's Chair in Chapter I or vice versa? Which assessment tools will the classroom use and which should the specialist administer? These are all questions that should be addressed to best support students with special needs.

Life always seems to get more hectic than usual when progress reports and conferences loom ahead. Specialists and teachers may decide to complete progress reports separately, then compare notes. Others may feel it would be more informative to bring samples of the student's work and fill out the progress report together. Some specialists may want to be a part of parent conferences in the classroom, particularly if they are student-led (Chapter 10). Much will depend on the individual child's needs, the type of program, and the level of comfort and trust within the staff.

Title the coral ror

Author Bob reese

thts is a cad Hoorads deurs mt

parriscult

Title Look out.8

Author Mavis Smith

socr i Like socr. I lost

red A book abawt socr

A boy crcsa ball throw

the windo. The ball

flovg throw the haws

and hit owmowst

evre thining in the haws.

name_____

date ~~eb 17 aa~~ APR 20 '93

Title the Bravest Dog T_____

Author By natalie

then the hunter
took his pack of wolfs

from were he was thay.

had to cras a freazing river

with out ice thay had

To cas it toget to the

sick children. then thay

came to the docter

the docter hored to the

children and gave them

ther medacin after a few

weeks the children were Betr

THE RESOURCE ROOM EVALUATION

Jan Peacoe designed the questionnaire on the next page to elicit information about the student's view of the Resource Room. You can easily adapt the form for an ESL, Chapter I, or enrichment program.

Weekly and Bi-Weekly Reports

Students with special needs often warrant additional observation and support. Some students may have difficulty socially, behaviorally, or academically. Fold the Weekly Progress Report (page 227) in half and ask the student to complete her/his evaluation for the week. Without looking at the student's responses, you then fill out the other half. Together you can then sit and compare perceptions. Students take the form home and parents comment on the space provided. You can file the completed Weekly Progress Report in your Teacher's Notebook. You'll probably want to modify the form to focus on particular areas of concern for each child.

The Bi-Weekly Report (page 228) is very similar and the ratings can be completed by the teacher and/or student. Like the previous form, room is provided for teacher, student, and parent comments. We have included a completed form as an example. The purpose behind these forms is to encourage students to evaluate their own behavior and to communicate with parents.

IDENTIFYING AND SETTING GOALS FOR STUDENTS WITH SPECIAL NEEDS

Most special programs require specific assessment or evaluation tools to meet federal or state guidelines. Much of the terminology does not reflect current research on learning and literacy acquisition. We've found, however, that there are ways to approach traditional and mandated forms that fit better with a whole language philosophy. All first grade teachers on Bainbridge Island use The Primary Initial Screening form (Chapter 6) to identify children who may qualify for special assistance. Children with low scores on this initial screening are assessed in more depth using standardized diagnostic tests and other tools described in this book.

Jan Peacoe developed the version of an Individual Educational Program (IEP) on page 230 for special education. Although terminology (behavior, objectives, proficiency) may not reflect her philosophy, Jan uses the concepts and language from the curriculum and continuum to describe student goals. Special education training at the college level and federal and state requirements are changing quickly. We hope they will soon reflect a more holistic view.

Much of what we know about our students won't fit on an IEP form. Good teaching is also a reflection of our sensitivity and intuition. Children with special needs are often anxious, afraid of failure, and afraid to take risks. Alfreda Furnas (1991), states, "I found my greatest challenge in teaching these students was one of the heart, not of the head" (p. 3). She adds, "As a teacher, my main task is simple. I must convince children in their hearts, that they *can* learn, and give them the skills to do it" (p. 4).

Resource Room Evaluation

Name_____ Date_____

Circle the words that tell how you feel and write comments in your own words.

1. I like going to the Resource Room.   **ALWAYS   SOMETIMES   NEVER**

2. I know what is expected of me
   in the Resource Room.   **ALWAYS   SOMETIMES   NEVER**

3. I am able to easily follow and
   understand my daily schedule.   **ALWAYS   SOMETIMES   NEVER**

4. The Resource Room teachers help
   me feel good about myself and learning.   **ALWAYS   SOMETIMES   NEVER**

5. The Resource Room has helped me with   **A LOT   A LITTLE   NOT AT ALL**
   my school work or to do better in my
   other class(es).

6. Please explain how the Resource Room has helped you or what could help you more.

   _____

   _____

7. If I could plan my own Resource Room program, I would _____

   _____

   _____

8. List what you like about the Resource Room: And what you don't like:

   _____   _____

   _____   _____

   _____   _____

   _____   _____

9. Choose the program you would like the best:

   a. Leave my classroom and come to the Resource Room.

   b. Stay in my classroom and have the Resource Room teachers come to help me.

WEEKLY PROGRESS REPORT

STUDENT'S SELF EVALUATION

	Always	Usually	Sometimes	Never
Comes to school prepared	1	2	3	4
Is on task	1	2	3	4
Does his/her best	1	2	3	4
Monitors own behavior	1	2	3	4
Cooperates with others	1	2	3	4

Student comments: _____

_____

_____

_____

Parent comments: _____

_____

_____

Date_____ Signatures: _____
(student)

WEEKLY PROGRESS REPORT

TEACHER'S EVALUATION

	Always	Usually	Sometimes	Never
Comes to school prepared	1	2	3	4
Is on task	1	2	3	4
Does his/her best	1	2	3	4
Monitors own behavior	1	2	3	4
Cooperates with others	1	2	3	4

Teacher comments: _____

_____

_____

_____

_____
(teacher)

_____
(parent)

_____'s Bi-Weekly Report for _____

(Name)   (Dates)

Area Evaluated	Rating	Comments (by teachers, student and/or parents)
Leadership		
Cooperation		
Reading		
Writing		
Thematic Studies		
Mathematics		

Rating Key

O = Outstanding Performance

M = Minimum Performance

N = Needs to Improve

_____ (Teacher's Signature)

_____ (Student's Signature)

_____ (Parent's Signature)

_____'s Bi-Weekly Report for _____

(Name)   (Dates)

Area Evaluated	Rating	Comments (by teachers, student and/or parents)
Leadership		
Cooperation		
Reading		
Writing		
Thematic Studies		
Mathematics		

Rating Key

O = Outstanding Performance

M = Minimum Performance

N = Needs to Improve

_____ (Teacher's Signature)

_____ (Student's Signature)

_____ (Parent's Signature)

Liam
(Name)

's Bi-Weekly Report for 4/12/93 → 4/23/93
(Dates)

Area Evaluated	Rating	Comments (by teachers, student and/or parents)
Leadership	+	Liam has shown positive, responsible leadership in the past
Cooperation	+	two weeks as well as working cooperatively with his groups instudies of ants and careers. Great job leading calendar!
Reading	M	A little too social at these times, perhaps our new seating
Writing	M	arrangement will help Liam's concentration and "at-task" behavior
Thematic Studies	M/+	Ants-had a little trouble focusing but now on his way. Careers - Great job modelling phone calling appointments
Mathematics	+	By improvement! Liam is really trying to do his best. He's setting his own goals & is challenging himself and doing work at an appropriate level for him.

Rating Key

O = Outstanding Performance

M = Minimum Performance

N = Needs to Improve

Cynthia & Ruptic
(Teacher's Signature)

Liam
(Student's Signature)

_____
(Parent's Signature)

Liam
(Name)

's Bi-Weekly Report for April 23rd - May 7th
(Dates)

Area Evaluated	Rating	Comments (by teachers, student and/or parents)
Leadership	+	Liam is leading with his good behavior as well as active participation in class discussions and projects
Cooperation	+	very cooperative and helpfully mature behavior
Reading	M	I would like to see Liam reading in a more focused way, especially with George's Marvelous Medicine began so long ago.
Writing	+	Liam has been much more invested in finishing his "Home Alone" story
Thematic Studies	+	Excellent job presenting final Arts project ...see Animal report to come!
* Mathematics	+	Liam has been very focused in math, especially with Pentominos

Rating Key

O = Outstanding Performance

M = Minimum Performance

N = Needs to Improve

Cynthia & Ruptic
(Teacher's Signature)

Liam
(Student's Signature)

_____
(Parent's Signature)

*Cindy is not here today, so we'll have to wait until Monday for Maths. Sorry

Individual Educational Program - IEP

ANNUAL GOALS AND INSTRUCTIONAL OBJECTIVES

Student _____ School _____ Grade _____

Service Area _____ Teacher/Therapist _____

Goal _____

(at least two instructional objectives should accompany each annual goal)

	Behavior	Proficiency	Measured by:	Projected Beginning	Projected Ending	Actual Completion
O B J E C T I V E S						

Parent Participation (Describe plans for parent participation in implementing student's Individual Education Program)

_____

_____

_____

Individual Educational Program - IEP

ANNUAL GOALS AND INSTRUCTIONAL OBJECTIVES

Student _____   School _Ordway_   Grade _1_

Service Area _Written Language_   Teacher/Therapist _Peacoe_

Goal _Chris will progress from an emergent to developing stage of writing by 10/93_

(at least two instructional objectives should accompany each annual goal)

Chris will... Behavior	Proficiency	Monthy Measured by:	Projected Beginning	Projected Ending	Actual Completion
O B J E C T I V E S					
use beginning and ending consonants in his writing	80%	Written Samples	10/92	10/93	3/93
read his own writing	80%	Written Samples	10/92	10/93	2/92
begin to use spacing between words	80%	Written Samples	10/92	10/93	2/92

Parent Participation (Describe plans for parent participation in implementing student's Individual Education Program)

_____

_____

CHAPTER THIRTEEN

Reporting Student Growth

Parents want to know three basic questions: "Is my child growing and learning?", "Is he/she growing at a rate appropriate for his/her age?" and "How can we help?" To answer the first question, teachers, students, and parents need to look at growth over time.

HOW DO WE KNOW STUDENTS ARE GROWING?

Some families keep a photo album filled with pictures of their growing children. Many families have a doorway where they carefully measure children every year. Parents smile nostalgically at outgrown baby clothes and children love to chuckle at stories about "when they were little." These family rituals are ways of marking growth.

As teachers, we also celebrate growth. We hang fall and spring self-portraits up side by side in the hall. We marvel at how a child's writing has improved since September and how many books a youngster has read. Students collect and select representative samples of their work in a portfolio to show how much they have learned. In our society, however, growth is not enough.

HOW DO WE KNOW STUDENTS ARE GROWING AT AN APPROPRIATE RATE?

Let's focus on the parents' second concern. Many parents can remember benchmarks for their children: walking and starting to say single words at around 12 months, becoming potty trained at around two, losing baby teeth in first grade, etc. Periodically parents take their children in for check ups and watch with interest as the doctor plots out where their children fall on the growth charts. New parents study baby books and mark developmental milestones on a calendar or call friends or relatives to report, "He just took his first step!" As siblings are born and children enter school, parents refer to baby books less often. They rely upon their growing experience and intuition about children's normal growth and development.

As teachers, we continually assess students throughout the day, collecting information informally, making observations, jotting down notes, and collecting work samples. At some point, however, teachers and students need to stop and evaluate their progress. For accountability purposes, we need to match the student's work against some kind of benchmark to discover if they are learning at a rate appropriate to their age level. The British Columbia document, *Supporting Learning* (1991), refers to these benchmarks as "widely-held expectations." Later in this chapter, we'll describe the continuum that the teachers on Bainbridge Island developed to address this issue.

HOW CAN WE HELP?

It's not enough to know how students are doing: we need to know where they are going next. Both parents and teachers need some sense of the "big picture." It's also important to know when a child is having difficulties. We need to learn specifically what activities and strategies can be used to support the child's next steps. The issue may simply be one of maturation and development. For instance, Philip may need many more experiences with familiar texts and predictable books before he is ready to focus on print. Both the teacher and Philip's family can continue to monitor his development, while pointing out letters in the environment and spending time each day reading aloud. Other children's areas for growth may require more specific support in particular areas. The most important thing for teachers is to focus on each child's strengths, yet to be honest with parents when there is a concern. Most parents want to help, but we need to be very clear about what strategies are most effective and how to support their children's learning in a positive and natural way.

The best task you can give to parents is to read to their children every night. There are very few facts that researchers agree on, but it is virtually undisputed that parents who read with their children at least ten minutes a night are giving them a tremendous gift. "The single most important activity for building the knowledge required for eventual success in reading is reading aloud to children." (p. 23, Anderson et al., 1985). Put this quote above your door and in parent newsletters. Reading aloud helps develop basic concepts about language and stories, improves vocabulary, and nourishes a love of reading. In addition, sharing books together is one of the most wonderful experiences families can share.

Most of the previous chapters provided information on assessing student learning. In this chapter, we will discuss the continuums, progress reports, learning portraits, and learning profiles that Bainbridge Island teachers developed for evaluating and reporting growth.

SOMETHING'S NOT RIGHT WITH THIS PICTURE

It's the week before parent conferences and stacks of report cards on NCR paper are squeezed into teachers' mailboxes. Teachers groan and mentally cancel movies and family outings for the next several nights. After school, they sit with conference notes, gradebooks, and scattered notes from parents, trying to fill out boxes in the behavior section of report cards. Children are given seatwork and instruction pauses so teachers can quickly assess students to fill in missing gaps for particular children. At night they lug home boxes of student journals and puzzle over how to squeeze all they know about a child's writing into little squares with a half-inch space for comments. What's worse, the terms don't reflect a process approach to teaching writing. The day before conferences, students wonder/worry and try to peek through sealed manilla envelopes. It's an all-too-familiar picture.

Many parents, students, and teachers are frustrated with the use of grades and traditional report cards. Many feel that grades foster a sense of competition and inequity. The criteria for grades are often unclear; a paper that might receive an "A" in one class could be a "B–" paper in another. In addition, grades are often perceived as external motivation. Finally, report cards don't really say much that was very meaningful. Teachers, parents, and students yearn for a way to report learning that is simple, understandable, and consistent.

Philosophy and curriculum have been changing on Bainbridge Island. Last year, the teachers decided it was time to bridge the gaps between philosophy, curriculum, and evaluation. Perhaps evaluation could actually mesh with current research and instruction in their classrooms.

CHANGES IN TEACHING READING AND WRITING

In recent years, the teaching of reading and writing has changed significantly. In whole language classrooms, teachers treat children as readers and writers from the first day of school. Teachers surround students with environmental print and varied opportunities to explore language. Recent research in literacy acquisition has clearly shown that reading and writing are developmental processes that begin almost from birth (Hall, 1987; Harste, Woodward & Burke, 1984; Morrow, 1989). Rather than viewing reading and writing as something to be "taught" in first grade, we now know that children acquire many concepts about print at an early age. Many two-year-olds can spot favorite restaurants and preschoolers often act like they are really reading the books they have memorized. Literacy learning, and indeed all learning, occurs on a continuum.

FIRST STEPS

"What can most second graders do as readers by the end of the year?" "What kinds of writing skills do most fourth graders demonstrate by June?" The teachers on Bainbridge Island met by grade level and began to talk about these and similar questions. Despite a wide range of experience and philosophy, the teachers could pinpoint common patterns for each age group. These benchmarks were then expanded into writing and reading continuums with specific descriptors for each developmental stage. The continuum initially consisted of eight stages of reading and writing development, with the recognition that there would be a range of developmental stages in any one grade. The continuums were later revised and expanded into nine stages which we'll describe shortly.

Many teachers on the Island were well-grounded in a whole language philosophy and had done extensive reading about process writing, integrated curriculum, and literature-based reading. In retrospect however, it was a validating and symbolic step to begin with the teachers' own experience and intuition instead of starting with the work of outside "authorities." The teachers first developed and refined rough benchmarks that they eventually formed into a continuum. Many teachers read additional research on emergent literacy and language development. Others explored new books on assessment and studied continuums that other districts had developed. Teachers also began noting patterns of growth in their own classrooms.

THE READING/WRITING CONTINUUM

The Bainbridge Island School District defines a continuum as "A visual representation of literacy development using descriptors to depict the developmental stages of learning." Patti Kamber's fifth-grade students provided more poetic definitions:

A continuum is a way to tell where you are in a process.

A continuum is a factual timeline of your learning and knowledge. It helps you keep track of your abilities.

A continuum is like your family; it goes on and on.

I like using a continuum because I like to know where I am, instead of ++, +, ✓+, ✓, or 4, 3, 2, 1.

A continuum is a timeline to show where you are in reading and writing. The four categories are expanding, fluent, proficient, and independent. There is no good or bad place. Everyone is different and more successful in different subjects.

A continuum is an everlasting list of where you are.

The Reading and Writing Continuums that the teachers on Bainbridge Island developed reflect concepts and terminology from the curriculum, such as process writing and literature-based reading. Parents were delighted with the clear language and specific descriptors. Teachers discovered that dating the continuum was easier than filling in boxes with numbers, particularly as they became more comfortable with the continuums. Many teachers had been using the checklists version from the continuum and assessment forms from this book during the daily course of instruction. These teachers found that transferring information to the progress report was relatively simple. The descriptors on the continuum are specific enough that teachers can be consistent and clear about the criteria for evaluation. Teachers, parents, and students now have a common language to use when talking about reading and writing development. In addition, the process of developing and revising the continuum became a vehicle for teachers to articulate and examine educational practices.

At each grading period, teachers simply place the month and year on the reading and writing continuums above the appropriate stage. The teachers intentionally did not place lines between the stages so that the date could be placed anywhere along the continuum. Many teachers also chose to highlight the specific descriptors on the continuum, using different colors for each grading period. One reason for using a continuum was to emphasize that learning is a process and that the emphasis should be on progress, rather than on competition. We want our children to be internally motivated lifelong learners.

How Did the Continuum Change?

As the teachers and students used the continuum the first year, they discovered the need for minor changes. A ninth stage was added and the descriptors were reordered and revised. The nine developmental stages are:

Pre-Conventional

Emergent

Developing

Beginning

Expanding

Bridging

Fluent

Proficient

Independent

The progress report for each grade level shows 5 stages from the continuum. We've included the continuums used in first through fifth grade. You can read the descriptors better on the checklist form later in this chapter. By using the Bainbridge Island continuums as a scaffolding, you can make changes to fit your own particular population and needs.

Reading Continuum

Preconventional	Emergent	Developing	Beginning	Expanding	Effort

• Holds book, correctly turns pages. • Chooses book and has favorites. • Shows start/end of book. • Listens and responds to literature. • Knows some letter names. • Interested in environmental print.	• Pretends to read. • Uses illustrations to tell stories. • Participates in reading of familiar books. • Knows most letter sounds. • Recognizes names/words in context. • Memorizes pattern books and familiar books. • Rhymes and plays with words.	• Sees self as reader. • Reads books with word patterns. • Knows most letter sounds. • Retells main idea of text. • Recognizes simple words. • Relies on print and illustrations.	• Reads early-reader books. • Relies on print more than illustrations. • Uses sentence structure clues. • Uses meaning clues. • Uses phonetic clues. • Retells beginning, middle, end. • Recognizes names/words by sight. • Begins to read silently. • Understands basic punctuation.	• Reads beginning chapter books. • Reads and finishes a variety of materials with frequent guidance. • Uses reading strategies appropriately. • Retells plot, characters, and events. • Recognizes different types of books. • Makes connections between reading, writing, and experiences. • Silent reads for short periods.	

Writing Continuum

Preconventional	Emergent	Developing	Beginning	Expanding	Effort

• Makes marks other than drawing on paper (scribble writing). • Primarily relies on pictures to convey meaning. • Sometimes labels and adds "words" to pictures. • Tells about own writing. • Writes random recognizable letters.	• Sees self as writer. • Copies names and familiar words. • Uses pictures and print to convey meaning. • Pretends to read own writing. • Prints with upper-case letters. • Uses beginning/ending consonants to make words.	• Takes risks with writing. • Begins to read own writing. • Writes names and favorite words. • Writing is from top-bottom, left-right, front-back. • May interchange upper and lower case letters. • Begins to use spacing between words. • Uses beginning, middle and ending sounds to make words. • Begins to write noun-verb phrases.	• Writes pieces that self and others can read. • Begins to write recognizable short sentences. • Writes about observations and experiences with some descriptive words. • Experiments with capitals and punctuation. • Forms many letters legibly. • Uses phonetic spelling to write independently. • Spells some words correctly. • Begins to revise by adding on.	• Begins to consider audience. • Writes pieces with beginning, middle and end. • Revises by adding description and detail. • Listens to peers' writing and offers feedback. • Edits for punctuation and spelling. • Uses capital letters and periods. • Forms letters with ease. • Spells many common words correctly.	

Reading Continuum

Emergent	Developing	Beginning	Expanding	Bridging	Effort
• Pretends to read. • Uses illustrations to tell story. • Participates in reading of familiar books. • Knows most letter sounds. • Recognizes names/words in context. • Memorizes pattern and familiar books. • Rhymes and plays with words.	• Sees self as reader. • Reads books with word patterns. • Knows most letter sounds. • Retells main idea of text. • Recognizes simple words. • Relies on print and illustrations.	• Reads early-reader books. • Relies on print more than illustrations. • Uses sentence structure clues. • Uses meaning clues. • Uses phonetic clues. • Retells beginning, middle, end. • Recognizes names/words by sight. • Begins to read silently. • Understands basic punctuation.	• Reads beginning chapter books. • Reads and finishes a variety of materials with frequent guidance. • Uses reading strategies appropriately. • Retells plot, characters, and events. • Recognizes different types of books. • Makes connections between reading, writing, and experiences. • Silent reads for short periods.	• Reads medium level chapter books. • Reads and finishes a variety of materials with guidance. • Reads and understands most new words. • Uses reference materials to locate information with guidance. • Increases knowledge of literary elements and genres. • Silent reads for extended periods.	

Writing Continuum

Emergent	Developing	Beginning	Expanding	Bridging	Effort
• Sees self as writer. • Copies names and familiar words. • Uses pictures and print to convey meaning. • Pretends to read own writing. • Prints with upper-case letters. • Uses beginning/ending consonants to make words.	• Takes risks with writing. • Begins to read own writing. • Writes names and favorite words. • Writing is from top-bottom, left-right, front-back. • May interchange upper and lower case letters. • Begins to use spacing between words. • Uses beginning, middle and ending sounds to make words. • Begins to write noun-verb phrases.	• Writes pieces that self and others can read. • Begins to write recognizable short sentences. • Writes about observations and experiences with some descriptive words. • Experiments with capitals and punctuation. • Forms many letters legibly. • Uses phonetic spelling to write independently. • Spells some words correctly. • Begins to revise by adding on.	• Begins to consider audience. • Writes pieces with beginning, middle and end. • Revises by adding description and detail. • Listens to peers' writing and offers feedback. • Edits for punctuation and spelling. • Uses capital letters and periods. • Forms letters with ease. • Spells many common words correctly.	• Begins to write for various purposes. • Begins to organize ideas in logical sequence. • Begins to develop paragraphs. • Begins to revise by adding literary devices. • Develops editing and proof reading skills. • Employs strategies to spell difficult words correctly.	

Reading Continuum

Developing	Beginning	Expanding	Bridging	Fluent
• Sees self as reader. • Reads books with word patterns. • Knows most letter sounds. • Retells main idea of text. • Recognizes simple words. • Relies on print and illustrations.	• Reads early-reader books. • Relies on print more than illustrations. • Uses sentence structure clues. • Uses meaning clues. • Uses phonetic clues. • Retells beginning, middle, end. • Recognizes names/words by sight. • Begins to read silently. • Understands basic punctuation.	• Reads beginning chapter books. • Reads and finishes a variety of materials with frequent guidance. • Uses reading strategies appropriately. • Retells plot, characters, and events. • Recognizes different types of books. • Makes connections between reading, writing, and experiences. • Silent reads for short periods.	• Reads medium level chapter books. • Reads and finishes a variety of materials with guidance. • Reads and understands most new words. • Uses reference information to locate information with guidance. • Increases knowledge of literary elements and genres. • Silent reads for extended periods.	• Reads most young adult literature. • Selects, reads and finishes a wide variety of materials. • Uses reference materials independently. • Understands literary elements and genres. • Begins to interpret deeper meaning in young adult literature with frequent guidance. • Participates in guided literary discussions.

Writing Continuum

Developing	Beginning	Expanding	Bridging	Fluent
• Takes risks with writing. • Begins to read own writing. • Writes names and favorite words. • Writing is from top-bottom, left-right, front-back. • May interchange upper and lower case letters. • Begins to use spacing between words. • Uses beginning, middle and ending sounds to make words. • Begins to write noun-verb phrases.	• Writes pieces that self and others can read. • Begins to write recognizable short sentences. • Writes about observations and experiences with some descriptive words. • Experiments with capitals and punctuation. • Forms many letters legibly. • Uses phonetic spelling to write independently. • Spells some words correctly. • Begins to revise by adding on.	• Begins to consider audience. • Writes pieces with beginning, middle and end. • Revises by adding description and detail. • Listens to peers' writing and offers feedback. • Edits for punctuation and spelling. • Uses capital letters and periods. • Forms letters with ease. • Spells many common words correctly.	• Begins to write for various purposes. • Begins to organize ideas in logical sequence. • Begins to develop paragraphs. • Begins to revise by adding literary devices. • Develops editing and proof reading skills. • Employs strategies to spell difficult words correctly.	• Uses appropriate tone and mood for a variety of purposes. • Experiments with complex sentence structure. • Connects paragraphs in logical sequence. • Uses an increased repertoire of literary devices. • Revises for clarity by adding reasons and examples. • Includes deleting in revision strategies. • Edits with greater precision (spelling, grammar, punctuation, capitalization).

Reading Continuum

Beginning	Expanding	Bridging	Fluent	Proficient	Effort
•Reads early-reader books. •Relies on print more than illustrations. •Uses sentence structure clues. •Uses meaning clues. •Uses phonetic clues. •Retells beginning, middle, end. •Recognizes names/words by sight. •Begins to read silently. •Understands basic punctuation.	•Reads beginning chapter books. •Reads and finishes a variety of materials with frequent guidance. •Uses reading strategies appropriately. •Retells plot, characters, and events. •Recognizes different types of books. •Makes connections between reading, writing, and experiences. •Silent reads for short periods.	•Reads medium level chapter books. •Reads and finishes a variety of materials with guidance. •Reads and understands most new words. •Uses reference materials to locate information with guidance. •Increases knowledge of literary elements and genres. •Silent reads for extended periods.	•Reads most young adult literature. •Selects, reads and finishes a wide variety of materials. •Uses reference materials independently. •Understands literary elements and genres. •Begins to interpret deeper meaning in young adult literature with frequent guidance. •Participates in guided literary discussions.	•Reads complex young adult literature. •Moves between many genres with ease. •Integrates non-fiction information to develop a deeper understanding •Interprets sophisticated meaning in young adult literature with guidance. •Participates in complex literary discussions.	

Writing Continuum

Beginning	Expanding	Bridging	Fluent	Proficient	Effort
•Writes pieces that self and others can read. •Begins to write recognizable short sentences. •Writes about observations and experiences with some descriptive words. •Experiments with capitals and punctuation. •Forms many letters legibly. •Uses phonetic spelling to write independently. •Spells some words correctly. •Begins to revise by adding on.	•Begins to consider audience. •Writes pieces with beginning, middle and end. •Revises by adding description and detail. •Listens to peers' writing and offers feedback. •Edits for punctuation and spelling. •Uses capital letters and periods. •Forms letters with ease. •Spells many common words correctly.	•Begins to write for various purposes. •Begins to organize ideas in logical sequence. •Begins to develop paragraphs. •Begins to revise by adding literary devices. •Develops editing and proof reading skills. •Employs strategies to spell difficult words correctly.	•Uses appropriate tone and mood for a variety of purposes. •Experiments with complex sentence structure. •Connects paragraphs in logical sequence. •Uses an increased repertoire of literary devices. •Revises for clarity by adding reasons and examples. •Includes deleting in revision strategies. •Edits with greater precision (spelling, grammar, punctuation, capitalization).	•Adapts style for a wide range of purposes. •Varies sentence complexity naturally. •Uses literary devices effectively. •Integrates information from a variety of sources to increase power of writing. •Uses sophisticated descriptive language. •Uses many revision strategies effectively.	

Reading Continuum

Effort

Expanding	Bridging	Fluent	Proficient	Independent
• Reads beginning chapter books. • Reads and finishes a variety of materials with frequent guidance. • Uses reading strategies appropriately. • Retells plot, characters, and events. • Recognizes different types of books. • Makes connections between reading, writing, and experiences. • Silent reads for short periods.	• Reads medium level chapter books. • Reads and finishes a variety of materials with guidance. • Reads and understands most new words. • Uses reference materials to locate information with guidance. • Increases knowledge of literary elements and genres. • Silent reads for extended periods.	• Reads most young adult literature. • Selects, reads and finishes a wide variety of materials. • Uses reference materials independently. • Understands literary elements and genres. • Begins to interpret deeper meaning in young adult literature with frequent guidance. • Participates in guided literary discussions.	• Reads complex young adult literature. • Moves between many genres with ease. • Integrates non-fiction information to develop a deeper understanding. • Interprets sophisticated meaning in young adult literature with guidance. • Participates in complex literary discussions.	• Voluntarily reads and under-stands a wide variety of com-plex and sophisticated materials with ease. • Evaluates, interprets and analyzes literary elements critically.

Writing Continuum

Effort

Expanding	Bridging	Fluent	Proficient	Independent
• Begins to consider audience. • Writes pieces with begin-ning, middle and end. • Revises by adding descrip-tion and detail. • Listens to peers' writing and offers feedback. • Edits for punctuation and spelling. • Uses capital letters and periods. • Forms letters with ease. • Spells many common words correctly.	• Begins to write for various purposes. • Begins to organize ideas in logical sequence. • Begins to develop paragraphs. • Begins to revise by adding literary devices. • Develops editing and proof reading skills. • Employs strategies to spell difficult words correctly.	• Uses appropriate tone and mood for a variety of purposes. • Experiments with complex sentence structure. • Connects paragraphs in logical sequence. • Uses an increased repertoire of literary devices. • Revises for clarity by adding reasons and examples. • Includes deleting in revision strategies. • Edits with greater precision (spelling, grammar, punctua-tion, capitalization).	• Adapts style for a wide range of purposes. • Varies sentence complexity naturally. • Uses literary devices effec-tively. • Integrates information from a variety of sources to increase power of writing. • Uses sophisticated descriptive language. • Uses many revision strategies effectively.	• Writes cohesive in-depth pieces. • Internalizes writing process. • Analyzes and evaluates written material in-depth. • Perseveres through complex writing projects.

One challenge in writing this book was that at the last minute we had to modify several forms based on the "old" continuum to match the new revisions. Fortunately, one premise of the book is that you can adapt the forms to meet your own needs. As we've stated before, you may not want to use the Bainbridge Island continuum just as it is anyway. We've shared the process of developing the continuum in the hopes that your school or district will make changes and develop assessment and evaluation tools based on your particular population and framework.

At the end of the first year of using the continuum, Cindy Ruptic graphed the reading and writing development of her first and second graders on a chart. She used a dot on the left to indicate each child's stage of writing development in the fall. In the spring, she made a second dot to indicate each child's stage of writing development and drew a line to connect the two dots. Her chart clearly showed the growth her students made in only five months! This technique provides Cindy with a graphic picture of reading and writing growth in her classroom that she can share with parents at Back to School night. If other teachers were to collect whole-class data, the information could be helpful as they looked at developmental patterns within and across grade levels.

Portraits of Learners

This year a group of three teachers from Bainbridge Island wrote a handbook to accompany the continuums and progress report. The handbook includes the district's philosophy of assessment and evaluation, definition of terms, and a description of how to use the progress report. It also includes the continuum, portraits of learners and a checklist for each stage of reading and writing development. Sandi Sater, Carrie Holloway, and Patti Kamber developed what they called "portraits" of readers and writers at the nine stages on the continuum. The language is very informal and concrete. You could probably place your students in one of these stages quite easily by reading these portraits. The addition of very specific examples will help many teachers in using the continuum.

Like the continuums, the portraits will be modified and revised next year after teachers have used them. Next year they also hope to add specific student samples of authentic reading and writing to illustrate each stage on the continuums. Connecting the continuum with actual samples will help clarify descriptors and ensure consistency in the district.

The Continuum Checklist

To make the continuums useful on an ongoing basis, descriptors for each stage were put in a checklist form. Teachers can include the checklists in children's reading and writing folders. We've included the checklists, but want to emphasize that no child will fall neatly into one stage. Most children will exhibit characteristics from two or even three stages. You may wish to date the box each trimester or when you first observe a particular behavior. We purposely did not put grade levels on these forms or the continuum to emphasize the fact that in any one grade, you will find children at a variety of stages. The emphasis should be on growth in writing and reading.

By letting children know specific characteristics of each stage, they become more aware of their own growth, and can use the language from the continuums in their reflections. Assessment no longer is a mysterious process that teachers "do" to students! Some students have even come up to teachers with samples of their work that demonstrate particular strategies or skills. The continuus profiles and checklists are also included on the accompanying packet of forms and the disk.

PORTRAITS OF WRITERS

Preconventional

At this stage the children play at writing (scribble writing) and make random letters. The children may add these "words" to drawing to build meaning about their pictures. They may tell lengthy stories about their pictures.

Emergent

These children see themselves as writers. They may write their names and some familiar words in a way that others may understand. One or two letters, usually initial or ending consonants, may represent a whole word. They often use letters to label pictures. They will pretend to read their own writing, often elaborating to make a story.

Developing

Students clearly attempt to write with some recognizable letters and perhaps a few familiar words. They will use beginning, middle, and ending sounds to make these words. For example, *learn* might be LRn. They often interchange upper- and lower-case letters. They begin to write noun-verb phrases such as MI DG PLS (My dog plays). Their work looks like writing. For example, the writing goes across the page and begins to include spacing. They are able to read their own writing aloud for at least a short time after writing, but later may not remember what they intended.

Beginning

Students write about immediate experiences that self and others can read. They begin to write recognizable short sentences with some descriptive words. They use some capitals and periods, but not always in the right places. Many letters are formed legibly. Some words are spelled phonetically, and some are correct. (Example: Once apon a tim ther wuz a Huntr he whent hunting evryday.) They often start a story with "Once upon a time" or finish with "The end." Children may revise by adding on.

Expanding

Students often write about their experiences and interests. They begin to consider audience by adapting the tone to suit their purposes. For example, in a Halloween story, word choice, characterization, and plot will be different when written for a kindergartener than for a peer. Pieces contain a beginning, middle, and end which may be elaborated with description and detail. They enjoy reading their stories and are able to offer specific feedback to peers. Their editing skills continue to grow, though are still fairly inconsistent. Students no longer labor over the physical act of writing. Many common words are spelled correctly, however, inconsistencies frequently occur.

Bridging

Students begin to develop and organize their ideas into paragraphs with teacher guidance. Students at this stage are able to write for an increasing number of purposes. This is a time of practice, and the writing is often uneven: the writer may focus on one aspect of the piece, but pay less attention to others. Students are learning that meaning can be made more precise through the use of details, reasons, and examples. Literary devices such as dialogue, similes, and alliteration are added during the revision process (usually with teacher guidance). Students edit their own and their peers' work with greater precision.

Fluent

This is a stage of increasing complexity. The writer has internalized appropriate tone and mood. For example, when given a teacher-directed assignment to write a biographical essay on a leader, the writer would know to use a serious tone. The writer attempts to vary sentence length and complexity. For example, they may start a sentence with an adverbial phrase ("Nervously, the boy sat at his desk, awaiting his turn to speak.") They also use transitions effectively, such as: however, and, but, and or. These writers have internalized a variety of literary devices. Writing is becoming more coherent and organized within paragraphs and in the connection of paragraphs. Revision strategies include providing examples, adding reasons, and deleting in order to clarify. In their editing, they find most of their own basic spelling, grammar, punctuation, and capitalization errors.

Proficient

This level is sophisticated. These writers often deal with abstract and complex issues in their writing. They are prolific and versatile. These writers show great flexibility in moving between teacher-directed and self-selected topics. These children show a willingness to revise and enjoy the art of writing.

Independent

These writers have internalized the writing process and persevere through extensive projects. These analytic writers may have their own distinctive style, but through their evaluation of written material, their style continues to grow.

PORTRAITS OF READERS

Preconventional

Preconventional learners display curiosity about books and reading. They enjoy listening to stories and have favorites. They also enjoy holding the book and turning pages. They may talk about the story and label and comment on the pictures. They are interested in environmental print such as favorite restaurant signs, traffic signs, and cereal boxes. These children know some letter names. Many go through this stage before kindergarten.

Emergent

Emergent learners are curious about reading and see themselves as potential readers. They may role-play themselves as readers. They rely on pictures to tell the story but are beginning to focus on print. During read-aloud, they may chime in with a familiar or predictable word or phrase. Also, after hearing pattern, rhyming, or predictable books many times, they may memorize them. They also may enjoy rhyming and playing with words. They will recognize familiar words such as their names or favorite places. They know some letter sounds. Children at this age are highly motivated and may move through this stage rather quickly.

Developing

Developing learners see themselves as readers and read simple word pattern books such as consonant-vowel-consonant word rhyming books. They know most letter sounds and recognize simple words such as: it, dog, cat, and, the, etc. They now merge print and illustrations to build meaning. They can retell the main idea of a story. This is another stage that children may pass through quickly.

Beginning

Beginning learners rely on print more than illustrations to create meaning. They understand basic punctuation such as periods, exclamations, and question marks. These students can read early-reader books such as *I Can Read* books or Dr. Seuss books. Later on in this stage they will read harder early-reader books such as *Little Bear* or *Frog and Toad* books. During silent reading time, these students may initially browse, but gradually are able to silent read for five minutes or more. They may take a developmental leap as they integrate reading strategies (sentence structure, meaning, phonetic clues). They know many words by sight. They are able to retell the beginning, middle, and end of stories. This is an exciting stage, however, it may take significantly longer to move through than earlier stages.

Expanding

This is a practicing and stretching stage. These students may read known and predictable favorites while also stretching into a variety of new materials. They may read beginning chapter books such as the *Polk Street Series*. They may also read non-fiction materials, comics, or magazines, such as *New True Books, Ranger Rick,* or *Garfield.* They now silent read for a longer period (ten minutes or more). They use a variety of reading strategies independently. These students may make connections between reading, writing, and experiences. For example, after hearing the story, *Charlotte's Web*, a child may be inspired to write about a special relationship. These students are also able to retell plot, characters, and events of stories they read or hear. They can recognize different types of books such as non-fiction, fiction, and poetry.

Bridging

This is a connecting stage where readers strengthen their skills by reading longer books that are no longer vocabulary controlled. These students read medium-level chapter books such as *Ramona* books or *James and the Giant Peach*. They may broaden their interests by reading a wide variety of materials such as *World* magazine, *Calvin and Hobbes*, *Eyewitness*, or *Explorer* books. They are able to silent read for twenty minutes or more. These children may be able to use reference materials to do a simple report. Their increased knowledge of literary elements and genres may allow them to describe a character's growth over time, understand the importance of the setting to a story, and compare and contrast books.

Fluent

This is a level of increased sophistication. These students can deal with issues and topics which are becoming more complex. These students can read most young adult literature such as *Hatchet, Snow Treasure,* and *From the Mixed-Up Files of Mrs. Basil E. Frankweiler*. They select and finish a wide variety of materials independently. These students participate in teacher-guided literary discussions.

Proficient

This level is sophisticated. These are avid readers who independently select challenging material such as the trilogy by Tolkien, *The Westing Game*, and unabridged classics. These readers can move between genres with ease, although they may have established strong preferences. They can become deeply involved in literary discussions. These students will seek out additional information after reading material of interest.

Independent

These prolific readers select material of a complex nature, such as *This Boy's Life, Watership Down,* and *The Martian Chronicles*. These readers evaluate, interpret, and analyze in depth.

Writing Continuum Checklist

Preconventional

			Makes marks other than drawing on paper (scribble writing)
			Primarily relies on pictures to convey meaning
			Sometimes labels and adds "words" to pictures
			Tells about own writing
			Writes random recognizable letters

Emergent

			Sees self as writer
			Copies names and familiar words
			Uses pictures and print to convey meaning
			Pretends to read own writing
			Prints with upper-case letters
			Uses beginning/ending consonants to make words

Developing

			Takes risks with writing
			Begins to read own writing
			Writes names and favorite words
			Writing is from top-bottom, left-right, front-back
			May interchange upper- and lower-case letters
			Begins to use spacing between words
			Uses beginning, middle, and ending sounds to make words
			Begins to write noun-verb phrases

Beginning

			Writes pieces that self and others can read
			Begins to write recognizable short sentences
			Writes about observations and experiences with some descriptive words
			Experiments with capitals and punctuation
			Forms many letters legibly
			Uses phonetic spelling to write independently
			Spells some words correctly
			Begins to revise by adding on

Expanding

			Begins to consider audience
			Writes pieces with beginning, middle, and end
			Revises by adding description and detail
			Listens to peers' writing and offers feedback
			Edits for punctuation and spelling
			Uses capital letters and periods
			Forms letters with ease
			Spells many common words correctly

Bridging

			Begins to write for various purposes
			Begins to organize ideas in logical sequence
			Begins to develop paragraphs
			Begins to revise by adding literary devices
			Develops editing and proofreading skills
			Employs strategies to spell difficult words correctly

Fluent

			Uses appropriate tone and mood for a variety of purposes
			Experiments with complex sentence structure
			Connects paragraphs in logical sequence
			Uses an increased repertoire of literary devices
			Revises for clarity by adding reasons and examples
			Includes deleting in revision strategies
			Edits with greater precision (spelling, grammar, punctuation, capitalization)

Proficient

			Adapts style for a wide range of purposes
			Varies sentence complexity naturally
			Uses literary devices effectively
			Integrates information from a variety of sources to increase power of writing
			Uses sophisticated descriptive language
			Uses many revision strategies effectively

Independent

			Writes cohesive in-depth pieces
			Internalizes writing process
			Analyzes and evaluates written material in-depth
			Perseveres through complex writing projects

Reading Continuum Checklist

Preconventional

			Holds book, correctly turns pages
			Chooses books and has favorites
			Shows start/end of book
			Listens and responds to literature
			Knows some letter names
			Interested in environmental print

Emergent

			Pretends to read
			Uses illustrations to tell story
			Participates in reading of familiar books
			Knows some letter sounds
			Recognizes names/words in context
			Memorizes pattern books and familiar books
			Rhymes and plays with words

Developing

			Sees self as reader
			Reads books with word patterns
			Knows most letter sounds
			Retells main idea of text
			Recognizes simple words
			Relies on print and illustrations

Beginning

			Reads early-reader books
			Relies on print more than illustrations
			Uses sentence structure clues
			Uses meaning clues
			Uses phonetic clues
			Retells beginning, middle, and end
			Recognizes names/words by sight
			Begins to read silently
			Understands basic punctuation

Expanding

			Reads beginning chapter books
			Reads and finishes a variety of materials with frequent guidance
			Uses reading strategies appropriately
			Retells plot, characters, and events
			Recognizes different types of books
			Makes connections between reading, writing, and experiences
			Silent reads for short periods

Bridging

			Reads medium level chapter books
			Reads and finishes a variety of materials with guidance
			Reads and understands most new words
			Uses reference materials to locate information with guidance
			Increases knowledge of literary elements and genres
			Silent reads for extended periods

Fluent

			Reads most young adult literature
			Selects, reads, and finishes a wide variety of materials
			Uses reference materials independently
			Understands literary elements and genres
			Begins to interpret deeper meaning in young adult literature w/frequent guidance
			Participates in guided literary discussions

Proficient

			Reads complex young adult literature
			Moves between many genres with ease
			Integrates non-fiction information to develop a deeper understanding
			Interprets sophisticated meaning in young adult literature with guidance
			Participates in complex literary discussions

Independent

			Voluntarily reads and understands a wide variety of complex and sophisticated materials with ease
			Evaluates, interprets, and analyzes literary elements critically

How Did the Continuum Fit with the Progress Report?

Many whole language teachers prefer a narrative progress report. We've found that the leap from a traditional report card to a narrative format may be overwhelming for many teachers and parents. An intermediate step might be to include some checklists and/or boxes as well as more room for comments. Some teachers are very apprehensive about writing remarks. We've found sections on writing narrative comments from *Supporting Learning* (1992, pages 9-11) and the *Resource Document* (1991, pages 75-82) from British Columbia very useful for staff inservices.

The reading and writing continuum comprise the bottom half of the district's progress report. The top half of the progress report is still fairly traditional, with boxes for behavior, math skills, and content area learning. Teachers tried to have the "key" match the district's philosophy by using four choices: not applicable/observed, guidance necessary, developing, or independent. In the next few years, teachers on Bainbridge will be examining more meaningful ways to report learning in math, social studies, and science.

Philosophy, goals, curriculum, assessment, evaluation, and reporting are beginning to fit together!

The Learning Profile

It's important to remember that learning does not take place in one-year increments. To reflect learning over a longer period, a Learning Profile or "mini-portfolio" was developed which would follow a student for six years, from kindergarten through fifth grade.

Last year, some teachers on Bainbridge Island piloted the Learning Profile. This year, the district will require that all kindergarten and first grade teachers complete a Learning Profile for each student. Additional grade levels will be required to maintain Learning Profiles each year.

The Learning Profile includes samples of the following from the six years the child attends school in the district:

- Self-Portraits
- Writing Samples (Fall and Spring)
- School Pictures
- Content Area Samples/Continuum
- List of Books Read/Reading Log
- Math Card/Continuum
- Reading/Writing Continuums
- Progress Report
- Self-Reflection Letter

One teacher gathered a group of parent volunteers to put colored tabs on the notebooks that separate each division. For example, all the child's self-portraits K–5 are in one section. Each year, a child and his/her teacher collect several representative samples of work to include in the Learning Profile. In order to keep this profile simple and not too overwhelming, the teachers began the first year by selecting one thing each month to include. For instance, each September and May the students would include a self-portrait. Besides the required items, teachers also date a broader continuum in the profile, once in the fall and again in the spring. On this full continuum, people will be able to graphically see growth from kindergarten through fifth grade. Teachers also note two favorite books that the child has read or enjoyed each year.

As teachers become more comfortable with the Learning Profile, they may decide to add more components, such as audiotapes of children reading or attitude surveys. As a parent,

Student Name _____

School _____

Data Entered _____

Learning Profile Checklist

Teacher		K	1	2	3	4	5
September	Self-Portrait						
October	Writing Sample						
November	Continuums						
December							
January	Photograph						
February	Content Area						
March	Writing Sample						
April	List of Books						
May	Self Evaluation						
June	Math Card Continuums Progress Report						

STUDENTS NAME _____

LEARNING PROFILE K-5

READING CONTINUUM

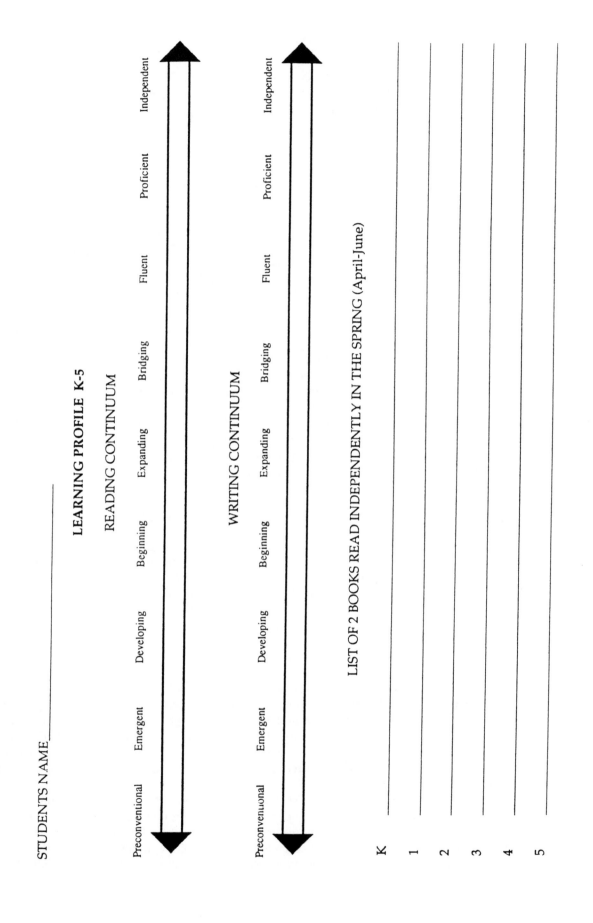

Preconventional Emergent Developing Beginning Expanding Bridging Fluent Proficient Independent

WRITING CONTINUUM

Preconventional Emergent Developing Beginning Expanding Bridging Fluent Proficient Independent

LIST OF 2 BOOKS READ INDEPENDENTLY IN THE SPRING (April-June)

K _____

1 _____

2 _____

3 _____

4 _____

5 _____

think how much fun it would be to have two portraits every year for six years, and to be able to see the changes and development over time! The Learning Profile is sent home with students when they leave the district or graduate from fifth grade.

INFORMING PARENTS

Parents need assurance that, since they have placed their child's education in your hands, you are doing a good job. Few parents are teachers themselves and many base their judgments and expectations on their own experiences in schools, whether negative or positive. The further you stray from a traditional mold, the more necessary it is to educate parents about the changes. Parents need reassurance that you are confident their child is learning and growing satisfactorily. You need to talk about changes such as the continuum and Learning Profile at Back to School Nights and curriculum nights. You may discover that 20-minute parent conferences are simply too short for you to share portfolios and describe the new continuums and progress report!

Most parents are eager to know specific ways in which they can support their child's learning at home. At the same time, you can talk about how you plan to help their child at school. The information you share with parents must also be supported by data. Anecdotal records, checklists, descriptors on the continuum, and your comments reveal much about how well you know their child. You can use research, your own classroom examples, and experience to show parents developmental patterns and benchmarks.

Teachers do more than just collect information. In the past, many teachers lugged boxes of student journals home the week before parent conferences, looked through piles of notes, and tried to match what they knew about children to boxes and grades on a report card. Assessment and evaluation are most effective when they occur naturally as part of ongoing classroom activities.

GRADING

On Bainbridge Island, the progress reports for elementary students do not have letter grades. Students are evaluated using the progress report and continuums. Teachers supplement this information with samples of student work and information from authentic assessment tools and techniques. Some of you may not be as fortunate. Robert Anthony and his colleagues (1991) write: "We believe that teachers should work collectively to negotiate with the administration the right to suspend the awarding of letter grades where appropriate. . . . there are much more effective ways than grades to make summative judgments about student achievement" (p. 142).

What if such negotiation is not yet possible in your school or district? How can you reconcile the assessment and evaluation approaches described in this book with having to "give grades"? What about the role of standardized tests? Our recommendation is to supplement the required grades and tests with more authentic measures. Attach a continuum and a narrative paragraph to the report card. Show parents the student's portfolios alongside the report card. Parents can become powerful advocates once they have seen examples of more authentic assessment and evaluation.

We also suggest that you involve students in developing the criteria for grading. As described earlier, you can set the *external* criteria, such as submitting three writing pieces to be "graded" each term. Students can revise and edit so that their writing reflects their best effort, then submit three pieces that show their growth as writers. Give students a voice in the process and help clarify expectations, whether you are using letter grades or not. Patti Kamber writes:

We consistently analyze learning activities in our classroom according to criteria we decide upon together. For example, when a writing assignment is given, we identify three or four criteria that we believe would make this a quality piece of writing. We put the criteria into writing. This is really where true learning about learning occurs. Putting the criteria in the open allows it to be analyzed by the learner and revised accordingly, while still meeting the teacher's responsibility. It removes the fuzziness from the learning process. Almost all the students meet or exceed the criteria.

After completing the assignment, students review their work using the selected criteria. They write a brief self-evaluation before conferring with me or a peer. Articulating the criteria to evaluate their work has been effective for all the children, particularly those of us who are not naturally intuitive. The greatest benefit of mutually setting criteria has been the opportunity to discuss and clarify what we value in education.

In order to evaluate students, we need to have clear criteria in mind, we must know each child in order to ascertain growth, and we must have some level of expectation in mind for the particular age of students we teach. We need to base our evaluation on clearly documented observations and student samples. Yet the amount of work students produce in a process-based classroom can be overwhelming. We can only assess and evaluate a small sample of what we *collect*. Evaluation requires that we *select* representative samples of a variety of types of products and processes to be evaluated. We also need to help children *reflect* on their learning. Ideally, this process becomes a continuous form of celebrating growth and setting goals for the future.

As professionals, part of our job involves reflecting on what we know about our students, making instructional decisions, setting goals, and then sharing that information with parents and administrators. You can convey this information to parents informally through newsletters and at curriculum presentations, Back to School Night, Portfolio Nights, and Author's Celebrations. You can communicate to parents informally through notes, conversations, and phone calls. Information about individual children can also be reported more formally through progress reports and at parent conferences.

CHAPTER FOURTEEN

Missing Pieces

As we worked on this book, the process of writing and revision helped us clarify parts of the puzzle. We realize, however, that many pieces are still missing. We didn't include forms or information about retelling, think-alouds, holistic or analytic scoring of writing. Our focus was limited to the elementary grades in a suburban district. The list of our limitations could go on and on. As the book kept getting longer and longer, our editor and families told us it was time to stop!

Our goal was to illustrate a wide variety of practical ways to assess and evaluate students. Many other techniques can be used to measure growth and inform instruction. Whether assessment is viewed as a puzzle, a box of tools, or a menu, the choices are up to you. What you decide to implement in your assessment program depends a great deal on your philosophy, your experience, and your beliefs about teaching and learning. There is no one "solution" to the puzzle. In her chapter in *Workshop 3: The Politics of Process*, Mem Fox states:

> No one has the right answers. It's more important to have the right questions. I believe that in order to teach real language successfully, you and I have only to understand the quality of *reality*, through personal observation and reflection, and to nurture its existence in our classrooms. "Is it real? Is it real? Is it real?" should be our daily educational mantra. If it were, and if we took notice of it in our teaching, we'd never again need to jump on anything so humdrum as bandwagons. Instead, we'd be in winged chariots, flying along the real language road toward the brilliant sunrise of universal literacy. (p. 45)

Teaching can be lonely. Surrounded by 20 to 30 noisy, energetic, exciting, and exhausting children, teachers seldom have times of quiet in which to work, or time to share and plan with colleagues. You probably arrive a few minutes early to gather what's needed for the day and work at your desk through lunch, reading journals and writing anecdotal comments. Teachers often stay late at school or rush off to take a class, and rarely have time to really talk with colleagues. Nowhere is this more evident than during staff inservices when the presenter can't get people to stop talking. It's not rudeness; it's a deep need for dialogue with other people who care about children. Many of you read the same novels, struggle with the same issues, and laugh over similar stories. You have probably developed forms much like the ones in this book. Yet you've probably done all this on your own.

In the first three chapters of this book we talked about the three stages teachers often go through when beginning to use portfolios: collect, select, reflect. What we'd like to add is the next step in professional growth: connect. The sharing among the teachers on Bainbridge Island as they met to talk about curriculum and assessment was revitalizing. Teachers at some grade levels who had never worked together have since become friends and true colleagues.

Teachers are sharing ideas, trying out each other's forms, writing articles, and presenting together at conferences. Salaries may not be higher or class sizes smaller, but teachers are enjoying teaching and learning more than ever before. They feel like professionals who are making a difference in the lives of the students they teach.

Some of you may have doubts about how changes in curriculum can take place in your school or district. Change takes time. Find one colleague in your school or start a support group in your district. Don't be overwhelmed by how much you're *not* doing! Focus on one or two new components to add to your program. Modify our forms and make changes until you and your students are satisfied, then add on. As Regie Routman (1991) says, you have to trust your intuition and be patient with yourself.

As you read this book, you may feel like we've been talking about your classroom. You may even wonder why your forms are so similar to ours. It's not surprising. We've probably been to the same conferences, read many of the same books, and been walking along the same path. We invite you to continue our interchange by using our forms and making changes as you discover what works best for you. We will continue to adapt and improve the forms ourselves. Please consider sending us your forms and modifications along with your name! We hope this book will be helpful as you develop your own practical aspects of authentic assessment.

References

Adams, M. (1990). *Beginning to read: Thinking and learning about print.* Urbana, IL: Center for the Study of Reading.

Airasian, P. (1991). *Classroom assessment.* New York, NY: McGraw-Hill.

Anderson, R., Heibert, E., Scott, J. & Wilkinson, I. (1985). *Becoming a nation of readers: The report of the commission on reading.* Washington, DC: National Institute of Education.

Anthony, R., Johnson, T., Mickelson, N., & Preece, A. (1991). *Evaluating literacy: A perspective for change.* Portsmouth, NH: Heinemann.

Atwell, N. (1987). *In the middle: Writing, reading, and learning with adolescents.* Portsmouth, NH: Heinemann.

Avery, Carol. (1993) *. . . And with a Light Touch: Learning about Reading, Writing, and Teaching with First Graders.* Portsmouth, NH: Heinemann.

Belanoff, P., & Dickson, M. (Eds.). (1991). *Portfolios: Process and product.* Portsmouth, NH: Heinemann.

Bickmore-Brand, J. (1990). *Language in mathematics.* Portsmouth, NH: Heinemann.

Bouffler, C. (Ed.). (1992). *Literacy evaluation: Issues and practicalities.* Portsmouth, NH: Heinemann.

Brown, H. & Cambourne, B. (1987). *Read and retell.* Portsmouth, NH: Heinemann.

Calkins, L. (1986). *The art of teaching writing.* Portsmouth, NH: Heinemann.

Camp, R. (1992). Portfolio reflections in middle and secondary school classrooms (pp. 61-79). In K. Yancy, *Portfolios in the writing classroom: An introduction.* Urbana, IL: National Council of Teachers of English.

Chittenden, E. (1991). Authentic assessment, evaluation, and documentation of student performance (pp. 22-31). In V. Perrone, *Expanding student assessment.* Alexandria, VA: Association for Supervision and Curriculum Development.

Clay, M. (1979). *The early detection of reading difficulties.* (Third Edition). Portsmouth, NH: Heinemann.

Clay, M. (1991). *Becoming literate: The construction of inner control.* Portsmouth, NH: Heinemann.

Clay, M. (1993). *An observation survey of early literacy achievement.* Portsmouth, NH: Heinemann.

Daly, E. (1989). *Monitoring children's language development: Holistic assessment in the classroom.* Portsmouth, NH: Heinemann.

Fein, S. (1993). *First drawings: Genesis of visual thinking.* Portsmouth, NH: Heinemann.

Fein, S. (1993). *Heidi's horse.* Portsmouth, NH: Heinemann.

Fisher, B. (1991). *Joyful learning: A whole language kindergarten.* Portsmouth, NH: Heinemann.

Flynt, E.S. & Cooter, R.B. (1993). *Reading inventory for the classroom.* Scottsdale, AZ: Gorsuch Scarisbrick Publishers.

Fox, M. (1993). *Radical reflections: Passionate opinions on teaching, learning, and living*. New York, NY: Harcourt Brace & Company.

Fryar, R., Johnston, N. & Leaker, J. (1992). Parents and assessment (pp. 99–110). In C. Bouffler (Ed.), *Literacy evaluation: Issues and practicalities*. Portsmouth, NH: Heinemann.

Fu, D. (1992). One bilingual child talks about his portfolio (pp. 171-183). In D. Graves & B. Sunstein (Eds.), *Portfolio portraits*. Portsmouth, NH: Heinemann.

Furnas, A. (1991). Yes, you can! (pp. 3-7). In Susan Stires (Ed.), *With promise: Redefining reading and writing for "special" students*. Portsmouth, NH: Heinemann.

Gentry, J.R. (1985). You can analyze developmental spelling, *Early Years K-8*, May.

Gentry, J.R. (1987). *Spel . . . is a four-letter word*. Portsmouth, NH: Heinemann.

Gentry, J.R. & Gillet, J.W. (1993). *Teaching kids to spell*. Portsmouth, NH: Heinemann.

George, J.C. (1988). *My side of the mountain*. New York, NY: Dutton.

Glazer, S. & Brown, C. (1993). *Portfolios and beyond: Collaborative assessment in reading and writing*. Norwood, MA: Christopher-Gordon Publishers.

Goodman, K. (1969). Analysis of reading miscues: Applied psycholinguistics. *Reading research quarterly, 5* (1), 652-658.

Goodman, K. (1981). *Miscue analysis: Applications to reading instruction*. Urbana, IL: National Council of Teachers of English.

Goodman, K., Goodman, Y., & Hood, W. (1989). *The whole language evaluation book*. Portsmouth, NH: Heinemann.

Goodman, Y. (1985). Kid watching: Observing children in the classroom (pp. 9-18). In A. Jagger & M.T. Smith-Burke (Eds.), *Observing the language learner*. Urbana, IL: National Council of Teachers of English.

Graves, D.H. (1983). *Writing: Teachers and children at work*. Portsmouth, NH: Heinemann.

Graves, D.H. & Sunstein, B.S. (1992). *Portfolio portraits*. Portsmouth, NH: Heinemann.

Hall, N. (1987). *The emergence of literacy*. Portsmouth, NH: Heinemann.

Harp, B. (Ed.). (1991). *Assessment and evaluation in whole language programs*. Norwood, MA: Christopher-Gordon Publishers.

Harste, J., Woodward, V. & Burke, C. (1984). *Language stories and literacy lessons*. Portsmouth, NH: Heinemann.

Heald-Taylor, G. (1989). *The administrator's guide to whole language*. Katonah, NY: Richard C. Owen Publishers.

Hubbard, R. (1989). *Authors of pictures, draughtsmen of words*. Portsmouth, NH: Heinemann.

Jacques, B. (1988) *Mossflower*. New York, NY: Philomel Books.

Jorgensen, K. (1993). *History workshop*. Portsmouth, NH: Heinemann.

Karelitz, Ellen B. (1993). *The Author's Chair and Beyond: Language and Literacy in a Primary Classroom*. Portsmouth, NH: Heinemann.

Leslie, L. & Caldwell, J. (1990). *Qualitative reading inventory*. New York, NY: HarperCollins Publishers.

Matthews, Cindy (1992). An alternative portfolio: Gathering of one child's literacies (pp. 158-170). In D. Graves & B. Sunstein (Eds.), *Portfolio portraits*. Portsmouth, NH: Heinemann.

Meyer, C. (1992). What's the difference between *authentic* and *performance* assessment? *Educational Leadership, 49* (5), 39-40.

Milliken, M. (1992). A fifth-grade class uses portfolios (pp. 34-44). In D. Graves & B. Sunstein (Eds.), *Portfolio portraits*. Portsmouth, NH: Heinemann.

Morrow, L. (1989). *Literacy development in the early years*. Englewood Cliffs, NJ: Prentice-Hall.

Newkirk, T. (1989). *More than stories: The range of children's writing*. Portsmouth, NH: Heinemann.

Perrone, V. (Ed.). (1991). *Expanding student assessment*. Alexandria, VA: Association for Supervision and Curriculum Development.

Peterson, R. & Eeds, M. (1990). *Grand conversations: Literature groups in action.* New York, NY: Scholastic.

Rhodes, L. (Ed.). (1993). *Literacy assessment: A handbook of instruments.* Portsmouth, NH: Heinemann.

Rhodes, L. & Dudley-Marling, C. (1988). *Readers and writers with a difference: A holistic approach to teaching learning disabled and remedial students.* Portsmouth, NH: Heinemann.

Rhodes, L. & Shanklin, N. (1993). *Windows into literacy: Assessing learners K-8.* Portsmouth, NH: Heinemann.

Rief, L. (1992). Eighth grade: Finding the value in evaluation (pp. 45-60). In D. Graves & B. Sunstein (Eds.), *Portfolio portraits.* Portsmouth, NH: Heinemann.

Roderick, J. (Ed.). (1991). *Context-responsive approaches to assessing children's language.* Urbana, IL: National Council of Teachers of English.

Romano, T. (1991). Prologue: Third Strike (pp. xvii-xviii). In Susan Stires (Ed.), *With promise: Redefining reading and writing for "special" students.* Portsmouth, NH: Heinemann.

Rosenblatt, L. (1978). *The reader, the text, the poem: The transactional theory of the literary work.* Carbondale, IL: Southern Illinois University Press.

Routman, R. (1991). *Invitations: Changing as teachers and learners K-12.* Portsmouth, NH: Heinemann.

Seger, F.D. (1992). Portfolio definitions: Towards a shared notion (pp. 114-124). In D. Graves & B. Sunstein (Eds.), *Portfolio portraits.* Portsmouth, NH: Heinemann.

Saul, W., Rearson, J., Schmidt, A., Pearce, C., Blackwood, D. & Bird, M. (1993). *Science workshop: A whole language approach.* Portsmouth, NH: Heinemann.

Schwartz, J. (1991). The intellectual costs of secrecy in mathematics assessment (pp. 132-141). In V. Perrone, *Expanding student assessment.* Alexandria, VA: Association for Supervision and Curriculum Development.

Sharp, Q. (Ed.). (1989). *Evaluation: Whole language checklists for evaluating your children.* New York, NY: Scholastic.

Shepard, L. (1989). Why we need better assessment. *Educational Leadership, 46* (4), 4-9.

Smith, F. (1988). *Understanding reading: A Psycholinguistic analysis of reading and learning to read.* Hillsdale, NJ: Lawrence Erlbaum Associates.

Stires, S. (1991). *With promise: Redefining reading and writing for "special" students.* Portsmouth, NH: Heinemann.

Strickland, D. & Morrow, L. (1989). *Emerging literacy: Young children learn to read and write.* Newark, DE: International Reading Association.

Teale, W. & Sulzby, E. (1986). *Emergent literacy: Writing and reading.* Norwood, NJ: Ablex Publishing Company.

Tierney, R., Carter, M., & Desai, L. (1991). *Portfolio assessment in the reading-writing classroom.* Norwood, MA: Christopher-Gordon Publishers.

Tunnell, M. & Ammon, R. (1993). *The story of ourselves: Teaching history through children's literature.* Portsmouth, NH: Heinemann.

Valencia, S. (1990). A portfolio approach to classroom reading assessment: The whys, whats, and hows. *The Reading Teacher, 43* (4), 338-340.

Walmsley, B., Camp, A. & Walmsley, S. (1992). *Teaching kindergarten: A developmentally appropriate approach.* Portsmouth, NH: Heinemann.

Watson, D. & Henson, J. (1993). Reading evaluation—miscue analysis (pp. 53-75). In B. Harp (Ed.), *Assessment and evaluation in whole language programs.* Portsmouth, NH: Heinemann.

Weaver, C. (1988). *Reading process and practice: From Socio-Psycholinguistics to whole language.* Portsmouth, NH: Heinemann.

Weeks, B. & Leaker, J. (1991). *Managing literacy assessment with young learners.* Evanston, IL: McDougal, Littell & Co. For information, contact Australian Press at 818-837-3755.

White, C. (1990). *Jevon doesn't sit at the back anymore.* New York, NY: Scholastic.

Wilde, S. (1989). Understanding spelling strategies: A kidwatcher's guide to spelling (pp. 227-236). In K. Goodman, et al., *The whole language evaluation book.* Portsmouth, NH: Heinemann.

Wilde, S. (1992). *You kan red this! Spelling and punctuation for whole language classrooms, K-6.* Portsmouth, NH: Heinemann.

Wood, A. (1984). *The napping house.* Orlando, FL: Harcourt Brace Jovanovich.

Yancey, K.B. (1992). *Portfolios in the writing classroom: An introduction.* Urbana, IL: National Council of Teachers of English.

ALTERNATE PUBLICATIONS

The Langley Evaluation Project: Two Districts Collaborate. For information, write James Kennedy Elementary School, 22259 48th Ave., Langley, British Columbia, Canada V3A 3Z7.

Language Arts Portfolio Handbook for the Primary Grades. (1993). Juneau School District, 10014 Crazy Horse Drive, Juneau, AL 99801. (907) 463-1967

Literacy Assessment in Practice: Language Arts. (1991). Education Department of South Australia. Distributed by The National Council of Teachers of English, Urbana, IL.

Literacy Profiles Handbook: Assessing and Reporting Literacy Development. (1990) and *English Profiles Handbook* (1991). School Programs Division, Ministry of Education, Victoria, Australia. In the United States, write to TESA, PO Box 382, Fields Lane, Brewster, NY 10509. (914) 277-8100

Student Friendly Guide to Writing with Traits. (1991). Northwest Regional Educational Laboratory, 101 S.W. Main, Suite 500, Portland, OR 97204-3297. (503) 275-9500

Supporting Learning: Understanding and Assessing the Progress of Children in the Primary Grades, Ministry of Education, 620 Superior St., Victoria, British Columbia, Canada. V9B 2M4 (604) 356-2500

Performance Assessment: Readings from Educational Leadership. (1992). Edited by Ronald S. Brandt. Alexandria, VA: Association for Supervision and Curriculum Development. The collection contains key articles on assessment from *Educational Leadership* by noted experts such as Rexford Brown, Dennie Palmer Wolf, and Grant Wiggins.

Literacy Assessment (1993). Edited by Eugene Jongsma and Roger Farr. The articles in this publication were reprinted from a themed issue of the *Journal of Reading, Vol. 36, No. 7.*

Bainbridge Island School District #303 Evaluation and Reporting Handbook, Grades Kindergarten - Fifth. (September, 1993). Bainbridge Island School District, 8489 Madison Ave. NE, Bainbridge Island, WA 98110-2999. (206) 842-2915

Checklist of Assessment Tools and Techniques

Student Portfolio

Now	Soon	Pages	Tool/Technique	Comments
		173–175	Interest Survey	
		205–208	Parent Survey	
		172	Self-Portrait	
		106, 148	Self-Evaluation of Portfolio Contents	
		193–198	Self-Evaluation Forms	
		47	Teacher Portfolio Review	
		37	Monthly Portfolio Letter	
			Friday Folder Form	
		171–187	Writing Attitude Survey	
		43	Writing Samples	
		77–83	Writing Folder Forms	
		97–101	"Fix-It" Writing Samples Fall/Spring	
		92, 94	10 Words Over Time (Spelling)	
		189	Spelling Attitude Survey	
		179–186	Reading Attitude Survey	
		121–128	Reading Log	
		130–132	Reading Folder Forms	
		147	Audio/Videotape of Reading	
		144	Reading Response Project Sample	
		141–145	Dialogue Journal Sample	
		133–141	Literature Circle Evaluation Sample	
		154–162	Content Area Projects Samples/Evaluation	
		190–191	Content Area Attitude Surveys	

Checklist of Assessment Tools and Techniques

Teacher Notebook

Now	Soon	Pages	Tool/Technique	Comments
		9	Philosophy and Goals	
		10	Curriculum and Assessment	
		173	General Information (phone numbers, etc.)	
		57–60	Anecdotal Records	
		83–89	Writing Conference Forms	
		63–72	Emergent Literacy Evaluation	
		237–241	Writing Continuum	
		247–249	Writing Checklists	
		109–114	Reading Conference Forms	
		237–241	Reading Continuum	
		247–249	Reading Checklists	
		117	Simplified Miscue Analysis	
		118	Running Record	
		49–51	Organizational Checklist	
		47	Portfolio Review (teacher)	
		200–201	Teacher Self-Evaluation/Report Card	

Index

ABOUT THE AUTHORS

Bonnie Campbell Hill received her Ph.D. in Reading/Language Arts from the University of Washington. She is at present an adjunct faculty member of Seattle Pacific University and Seattle University in addition to being an educational consultant. She has also taught elementary school in both Colorado and Washington.

Cynthia A. Ruptic is a member of the multi-age primary team at Blakely School on Bainbridge Island, WA. During 1993–1994, she is working as a teacher and consultant in Japan. She has also taught at the elementary and junior high school levels.

Pictured below are some of the teachers from Bainbridge Island, WA, who helped develop the materials presented in this book.

Left to Right: Sandi Sater, Jan Peacoe, Jan Colby, Roz Duthie, Mary Hadley, Carrie Holloway, Lisa Norwick, Karin Torgerson, Patti Kamber, and Roger Sater